Spicy

next

Please note that the cup and spoon measurements
used in this book are metric. A conversion chart
appears on page 128.

First published in Great Britain in 2008 by ACP Magazines Ltd.
This edition published in 2008 exclusively for Next Retail Limited.

next.co.uk
nextflowers.co.uk

ISBN 978-1-903777-33-6

Printed and bound in China

contents

starters and soups

duck & green onion gyoza

preparation time 40 minutes ■ cooking time 20 minutes
■ makes 30

1kg chinese barbecued duck

4 spring onions, sliced thinly

1 tablespoon japanese soy sauce

2 tablespoons cooking sake

2cm piece fresh ginger (10g), grated

1 fresh long red chilli, chopped finely

30 gyoza wrappers

2 tablespoons vegetable oil

sake dipping sauce

¼ cup (60ml) cooking sake

2 tablespoons japanese soy sauce

1 tablespoon lime juice

1 teaspoon caster sugar

1   Remove and discard skin and bones from duck; chop meat finely. Combine duck, onion, sauce, sake, ginger and chilli in medium bowl.

2   Place one heaped teaspoon of duck mixture in centre of each wrapper; wet edge around one half of wrapper. Pleat to seal.

3   Cover base of large frying pan with water; bring to a boil then add gyoza, in batches. Reduce heat, simmer, covered, 3 minutes.

4   Meanwhile, make sake dipping sauce.

5   Heat oil in same cleaned pan; cook gyoza on one side only, uncovered, in batches, until browned and slightly crisp. Drain on absorbent paper. Serve immediately with sake dipping sauce.

■ **sake dipping sauce** Combine ingredients in screw-top jar; shake well.

fajitas

preparation time 30 minutes ■ cooking time 15 minutes
■ serves 4

3 cloves garlic, crushed

¼ cup (60ml) lemon juice

2 teaspoons ground cumin

1 tablespoon olive oil

600g beef strips

1 large red pepper (350g), sliced thickly

1 large green pepper (350g), sliced thickly

1 medium yellow pepper (200g), sliced
thickly

1 large red onion (300g), sliced thickly

8 large flour tortillas

tomato salsa

2 medium tomatoes (300g), deseeded,
chopped finely

1 fresh long red chilli, chopped finely

½ cup coarsely chopped fresh coriander

1 clove garlic, crushed

1 small white onion (80g), chopped finely

2 tablespoons lime juice

1 Combine garlic, juice, cumin and oil in large bowl; add
beef, stir to coat in mixture. Cover; refrigerate until required.
2 Make salsa cruda.
3 Cook beef, in batches, in heated oiled large frying pan,
stirring, until browned all over and cooked as desired. Cover
to keep warm. Cook peppers and onion, in batches, in same
pan, stirring, until softened.
4 Meanwhile, heat tortillas according to instructions.
5 Return beef and pepper mixture to pan; stir gently over
medium heat until hot. Divide fajita mixture among serving
plates; serve with tortillas and salsa cruda and, if desired,
guacamole.

■ tomato salsa Combine ingredients in small bowl.

beef & bean tacos

preparation time 15 minutes ■ cooking time 20 minutes ■ serves 4

2 cloves garlic, crushed

400g minced beef

1 teaspoon chilli powder

1 teaspoon ground cumin

2 x 300g cans red kidney beans, rinsed, drained

⅓ cup tomato paste

1 cup (250ml) water

2 medium tomatoes (380g), chopped coarsely

8 taco shells

½ small iceberg lettuce, shredded finely

salsa cruda

½ cucumber (130g), chopped finely

1 small red onion (80g), chopped finely

2 small tomatoes (260g), seeded, chopped finely

2 teaspoons mild chilli sauce

1 Preheat oven to moderate (180°C/160°C fan-assisted).

2 Heat lightly oiled large non-stick frying pan; cook garlic and beef, stirring, until beef is browned all over. Add chilli, cumin, beans, paste, the water and tomato; cook, covered, over low heat about 15 minutes or until mixture thickens slightly.

3 Meanwhile, toast taco shells, upside down and uncovered, on oven tray in oven for 5 minutes.

4 Just before serving, fill shells with beef mixture, lettuce and salsa cruda.

■ **salsa cruda** Combine ingredients in small bowl.

vegetable pakoras

¾ cup (100g) besan (chickpea flour)

¼ cup (35g) self-raising flour

2 teaspoons ground cumin

1 teaspoon garam masala

¼ teaspoon ground turmeric

½ teaspoon chilli powder

2 teaspoons salt

2 cloves garlic, crushed

¾ cup (180ml) water, approximately

1 cup (100g) cauliflower florets

1 cup (85g) broccoli florets

vegetable oil, for deep-frying

1 small aubergine (230g), sliced

2 medium courgettes (240g), sliced

yogurt mint dipping sauce

2 tablespoons bottled mint jelly

¾ cup (180ml) natural yogurt

1 small red chilli, finely chopped

preparation time 20 minutes (plus refrigeration time) ■ **serves 4–6**

1 Combine all yogurt mint dipping sauce ingredients in small bowl; cover, refrigerate 1 hour.

2 Sift both flours, spices and salt into a medium bowl. Add garlic; whisk in enough water to make a thick batter. Cover; refrigerate 30 minutes.

3 Boil, steam or microwave cauliflower and broccoli, separately, until just tender; refresh under cold water, drain on absorbent paper.

4 Heat oil in large saucepan. Dip vegetable pieces, one at a time, into batter, drain away excess batter; deep-fry until browned lightly and crisp. Drain on absorbent paper. Repeat process with remaining vegetables. Serve with yogurt mint dipping sauce.

1½ cups (225g) plain flour
2 teaspoons salt
2 tablespoons vegetable oil
⅓ cup (80ml) warm water, approx.
vegetable oil, for deep-frying

chilli beef filling

2 tablespoons vegetable oil
1 medium onion (150g), chopped
2 cloves garlic, crushed
2 teaspoons grated fresh ginger
½ teaspoon dried chilli flakes
2 teaspoons ground coriander
2 teaspoons garam masala
1 teaspoon ground turmeric
1 teaspoon sweet paprika
500g minced beef
2 tablespoons lemon juice
¼ cup chopped fresh mint

sweet potato filling

3 small sweet potatoes (750g)
1 tablespoon vegetable oil
1 medium onion (150g), chopped
2 teaspoons cumin seeds
½ teaspoon black mustard seeds
1 long green chilli, chopped
2 cloves garlic, crushed
2 teaspoons grated fresh ginger
¼ teaspoon ground nutmeg
1 tablespoon lime juice
¼ cup chopped fresh coriander

meat & vegetable samosas

preparation time 30 minutes (plus standing time) ■ the pastry and each filling is enough for 28 samosas

1   Sift flour and salt into medium bowl; make well in the centre of flour, then add the 2 tablespoons of oil with just enough water to make a firm dough.
2   Knead dough on floured surface until smooth and elastic; form into a ball. Cover with cling film; stand at room temperature for 30 minutes.
3   Meanwhile, make chilli beef filling or make sweet potato filling.
4   Divide dough into 14 equal pieces; roll each piece into a 14cm x 20cm oval, then cut oval in half widthways. Repeat process, keeping the remaining pieces covered to prevent drying out.
5   Brush edges of each half-oval with a little water; fold into cone shape. Fill with heaped tablespoon of filling; press edges together to seal. Repeat with remaining dough and filling.
6   Deep-fry samosas in hot oil, in batches, until browned and crisp; drain on absorbent paper.

■ chilli beef filling Heat oil in large frying pan; cook onion, stirring, until browned lightly. Add garlic, ginger, chilli and spices; cook, stirring, until fragrant. Add minced beef; cook, stirring, until well browned. Remove from heat, stir in juice and mint; cool.

■ sweet potato filling Cook sweet potatoes until just tender, drain; cool. Cut each sweet potato into 1cm pieces. Heat oil in frying pan; cook onion, stirring, until soft. Add seeds, chilli, garlic, ginger and nutmeg; cook, stirring, until fragrant. Remove from heat, stir in sweet potato, juice and coriander; cool.

spicy mixed nuts

makes about 4 cups

2 tablespoons vegetable oil

1 cup (150g) raw peanuts

1 cup (150g) raw cashews

1 cup (150g) shelled pistachios

1 cup (160g) blanched almonds

2 teaspoons garam masala

½ teaspoon hot chilli powder

1 teaspoon salt

1   Heat oil in frying pan; cook the peanuts, stirring, until browned lightly; drain on absorbent paper. Repeat with remaining nuts.

2   Cook spices in same pan, stirring, until fragrant. Combine spices with nuts and salt in large bowl; cool.

tortilla lime soup

preparation time 20 minutes ■ cooking time 25 minutes ■ serves 4

1 medium white onion (150g), chopped coarsely

2 cloves garlic, quartered

1 fresh long red chilli, chopped coarsely

4 medium tomatoes (600g), peeled, quartered

1 tablespoon groundnut oil

¼ teaspoon ground allspice

1½ cups (375ml) chicken stock

1.25 litres (5 cups) water

2 teaspoons grated lime rind

¼ cup (60ml) lime juice

¼ cup (70g) tomato paste

⅓ cup (80ml) groundnut oil, extra

6 corn tortillas, cut into 2cm-wide strips

1 medium avocado (250g), chopped finely

2 spring onions, chopped finely

¼ cup coarsely chopped fresh coriander

1   Blend or process white onion, garlic, chilli and tomato until pureed.

2   Heat oil in large saucepan; cook tomato mixture and allspice, stirring, until fragrant.

3   Add stock, the water, rind, juice and paste. Bring to a boil then reduce heat; simmer, uncovered, about 15 minutes or until mixture thickens.

4   Meanwhile, heat extra oil in medium frying pan; cook tortilla strips in batches, until golden. Drain on absorbent paper. Divide tortilla strips among bowls; ladle soup over. Top with combined avocado, spring onion and coriander.

prawn laksa

preparation time 30 minutes ■ cooking time 45 minutes ■ serves 4

1 Make laksa paste.

2 Heat oil in large saucepan; cook laksa paste, stirring, about 5 minutes or until fragrant. Add coconut milk, stock, sugar, sauce and lime leaves; bring to a boil. Reduce heat; simmer, covered, 30 minutes.

3 Meanwhile, shell and devein prawns, leaving tails intact.

4 Place egg noodles in medium heatproof bowl, cover with boiling water; separate with fork, drain. Place rice noodles in same bowl, cover with boiling water; stand until just tender, drain.

5 Add prawns to laksa; cook, uncovered, until just changed in colour.

6 Divide noodles among serving bowls; ladle hot laksa into bowls. Top with sprouts and coriander; serve with lime.

■ **laksa paste** Blend or process ingredients until mixture forms a smooth paste.

---

1 tablespoon vegetable oil

2 x 400ml cans coconut milk

1 litre (4 cups) chicken stock

1 tablespoon brown sugar

2 teaspoons fish sauce

6 fresh kaffir lime leaves, shredded finely

1kg uncooked medium king prawns

250g fresh thin egg noodles

125g dried thin rice noodles

1 cup (80g) bean sprouts

¼ cup loosely packed fresh coriander leaves

1 lime, quartered

laksa paste

1 medium brown onion (150g), chopped coarsely

⅓ cup (80ml) coconut milk

2 tablespoons lime juice

1 tablespoon shrimp paste

2cm piece fresh ginger (10g), grated

1 tablespoon macadamias (10g), halved

10cm stick fresh lemongrass (20g), chopped finely

4 cloves garlic, quartered

2 fresh small red thai chillies, chopped coarsely

2 teaspoons ground coriander

2 teaspoons ground cumin

1 teaspoon ground turmeric

dhal & spinach soup

2 teaspoons cumin seeds

2 teaspoons coriander seeds

1 tablespoon ghee

2 medium onions (300g), chopped

2 cloves garlic, crushed

1 tablespoon grated fresh ginger

2 dried red chillies, chopped

8 curry leaves, torn

2 teaspoons black mustard seeds

½ teaspoon fenugreek seeds

1 teaspoon ground turmeric

tiny pinch asafoetida powder

1 cup (200g) masoor dhal (red lentils), rinsed, drained

2 medium potatoes (400g), chopped

1.25 litres (5 cups) chicken stock

1kg spinach, roughly chopped

2 tablespoons tamarind concentrate

¾ cup (100g) coconut milk powder

1 cup (250ml) boiling water

preparation time 20 minutes ▦ cooking time 20 minutes ▦ serves 6 to 8

1 Cook cumin and coriander seeds, stirring, in dry frying pan until fragrant. Blend or process until crushed.

2 Heat ghee in large saucepan; cook onions, garlic, ginger, chillies, curry leaves, mustard and fenugreek seeds, stirring until onions are browned lightly. Add crushed spices, turmeric and asafoetida; cook, stirring, 1 minute.

3 Add dhal, potatoes and stock to pan; bring to boil then simmer, covered, 15 minutes or until potatoes are tender. Stir in spinach; cook 2 minutes.

4 Blend or process soup mixture, in batches, until smooth; return to pan.

5 Add tamarind and blended coconut milk powder and water; stir until soup is thoroughly heated through.

1 tablespoon ghee

1 large onion (200g), chopped

4 cloves garlic, crushed

2 teaspoons finely grated fresh
ginger

2 small green chillies, chopped
finely

¼ teaspoon ground cinnamon

¼ teaspoon ground cloves

2 teaspoons ground coriander

1½ teaspoons ground cumin

1 teaspoon ground turmeric

4 cardamom pods, bruised

5 curry leaves

1 medium carrot (120g), chopped

1 medium apple (150g), chopped

1 large potato (300g), chopped

1 cup (200g) masoor dhal (red
lentils), rinsed, drained

1 litre (4 cups) chicken stock

1 tablespoon tamarind concentrate

1 tablespoon lemon juice

2 cups (500ml) coconut milk

2 tablespoons chopped fresh
coriander

mulligatawny soup

preparation time 20 minutes ■ cooking time 15 minutes
■ serves 6

1 Heat ghee in large saucepan, add onion, garlic, ginger, chillies,
all spices and curry leaves; cook, stirring, until onion is browned
lightly and mixture is fragrant.

2 Add carrot, apple, potato, dhal and stock to pan; simmer,
covered, 15 minutes or until vegetables are just tender. Discard
pods and leaves.

3 Blend or process soup mixture, in batches, until smooth; return
to pan. Add tamarind, juice, coconut milk and coriander; stir until
heated through.

relishes & salsas

chicken & yellow bean relish

preparation time 10 minutes ■ cooking time 10 minutes ■ makes 1 cup

3 cloves garlic, quartered

2 purple shallots (50g), chopped coarsely

1 tablespoon vegetable oil

2 tablespoons yellow bean paste

150g minced chicken

⅓ cup (80ml) coconut cream

2 tablespoons chicken stock

¼ teaspoon dried chilli flakes

⅓ cup loosely packed fresh coriander leaves

⅓ cup coarsely chopped fresh mint

1   Using mortar and pestle, crush garlic and shallot until mixture forms a paste.

2   Heat oil in wok; stir-fry garlic mixture until browned lightly. Add paste; stir-fry until fragrant.

3   Add minced chicken to wok; stir-fry until cooked through. Add coconut cream, stock and chilli; bring to a boil. Reduce heat; simmer, uncovered, about 5 minutes or until thickened. Remove from heat; stir in herbs.

4   Serve relish with sliced cucumber and carrot sticks, if you like.

black bean salsa

preparation time 15 minutes (plus standing time) ■
cooking time 20 minutes ■ makes 4 cups

¾ cup (150g) dried black beans, cooked

2 medium red peppers (400g), roasted,
peeled, sliced thinly

2 cups frozen corn kernels

1 small red onion (100g), chopped finely

1 fresh long red chilli, chopped finely

⅓ cup coarsely chopped fresh coriander

2 cloves garlic, crushed

2 tablespoons olive oil

1 tablespoon finely grated lime rind

½ cup (125ml) lime juice

1 teaspoon ground cumin

1   Place beans in small bowl, cover with water; stand
overnight. Drain.
2   Place beans in medium saucepan of boiling water. Return
to a boil, then reduce heat; simmer, uncovered, about 15
minutes or until beans are just tender. Drain.
3   Combine beans with remaining ingredients in large bowl.

tip   Goes well with grilled lamb chops; chicken and
cheese tostadas.

char-grilled pepper & green olive salsa

preparation time 15 minutes ■ **cooking time 10 minutes**
■ **makes 2 cups**

2 cups (240g) pitted green olives, chopped coarsely
150g char-grilled red pepper, drained
1 small red onion (100g), chopped finely
1 tablespoon lime juice
⅓ cup coarsely chopped fresh coriander

1   Blend or process half of olives until smooth. Transfer to medium bowl; stir in pepper, remaining olives, onion, juice and coriander.

tip Goes well with grilled lamb fillets; as a dip with warm tortillas; or on an antipasti platter.

banana & coconut sambal

makes about 2 cups

2 firm bananas, sliced
1 tablespoon lemon juice
1 teaspoon sugar
¼ teaspoon salt
1 small red chilli, chopped finely
¼ cup (20g) shredded coconut

Combine all ingredients in medium bowl; stir until well combined. Serve immediately.

tomato & mint kachumber

serves 4 to 6

4 medium tomatoes (760g)
1 medium onion (150g), sliced
¼ cup shredded fresh mint
¼ cup (60ml) lemon juice
2 teaspoons sugar
1 teaspoon salt

Peel and quarter tomatoes; discard seeds, then cut tomatoes into thin slices. Combine tomatoes, onion and mint in large bowl. Whisk juice, sugar and salt together in small, bowl then mix into tomato mixture. Cover; refrigerate at least 30 minutes.

cucumber & mint raita

makes about 1¼ cups

½ medium cucumber (150g)
1 teaspoon ghee
¼ teaspoon cumin seeds
¼ teaspoon black mustard seeds
¼ teaspoon ground cumin
1 cup (250ml) yogurt
1 tablespoon lemon juice
1 clove garlic, crushed
¼ teaspoon cayenne pepper
1 tablespoon chopped fresh mint

Peel cucumber; chop coarsely. Heat ghee in small pan; cook seeds and cumin, stirring, until seeds pop; cool. Combine spice mixture with cucumber, yogurt, juice, garlic and pepper in small bowl. Cover; refrigerate at least 2 hours. Just before serving, gently stir in mint.

date & tamarind chutney

makes about 2½ cups

75g dried tamarind

2 cups (500ml) boiling water

2 teaspoons vegetable oil

2 teaspoons black mustard seeds

2 teaspoons cumin seeds

500g fresh dates, pitted, chopped

¼ cup (60ml) malt vinegar

Combine tamarind and the boiling water in medium bowl; stand 30 minutes. Strain over bowl, pressing to extract all liquid; discard tamarind. Heat oil in small pan; cook seeds, stirring, until they pop. Combine dates with tamarind liquid, seeds and vinegar in medium pan. Simmer, uncovered, 5 minutes until mixture is almost dry. Blend or process until almost smooth. Spoon into hot sterilised jars, seal while hot.

spinach raita

makes about 2 cups

500g spinach

1 tablespoon ghee

1 small onion (80g), chopped finely

½ teaspoon black mustard seeds

1 teaspoon cumin seeds

1 teaspoon ground cumin

¼ teaspoon chilli powder

2 teaspoons lemon juice

1 teaspoon salt

2 teaspoons chopped fresh mint

1⅓ cups (330ml) yogurt

Cook spinach until wilted; drain, cool. Squeeze out excess liquid; shred. Heat ghee in small pan; cook onion, stirring, until lightly browned. Add seeds; cook, stirring, until seeds pop. Add remaining spices; cook, stirring, until fragrant. Add juice; cool. Combine salt, mint and yogurt in medium bowl; mix in spinach mixture.

carrot & sultana sambal

makes about 3 cups

2 teaspoons vegetable oil

1 tablespoon black mustard seeds

½ cup (45g) shredded coconut

2 large carrots (360g), grated finely

½ cup (80g) sultanas

¼ cup (60ml) lemon juice

⅓ cup chopped fresh mint

Heat oil in small saucepan; cook seeds and coconut, stirring, until coconut just starts to brown. Combine the coconut mixture with remaining ingredients in medium bowl; mix well.

tomato kasaundi

makes about 3 cups

4 large tomatoes (1kg), chopped

1 medium onion (150g), chopped

4 cloves garlic, chopped

1 tablespoon sliced fresh ginger

4 small red chillies, chopped

2 teaspoons salt

2 teaspoons ground cumin

½ teaspoon ground turmeric

½ teaspoon chilli powder

¼ teaspoon ground cloves

2 tablespoons vegetable oil

¼ cup (60ml) white vinegar

⅓ cup (75g) sugar

Blend or process all ingredients until pureed. Transfer mixture to large pan; stir, without boiling, until sugar is dissolved. Bring to boil; immediately simmer, uncovered, 45 minutes, stirring occasionally, or until mixture is thickened slightly.

coconut coriander chutney

serves 4 to 6

1 tablespoon ghee

1 teaspoon black mustard seeds

2 teaspoons cumin seeds

1 teaspoon garam masala

2 curry leaves, torn

1½ cups (135g) shredded coconut

2 small green chillies, chopped

½ teaspoon salt

¼ cup fresh coriander leaves

1 clove garlic, crushed

½ cup (125ml) coconut milk

¼ cup (60ml) lime juice

Heat ghee in small frying pan; cook seeds and garam masala, stirring, until fragrant. Stir in curry leaves. Blend or process remaining ingredients until pureed; combine with spice mixture in medium bowl. Shape into a 12cm round on a serving plate.

sweet mango chutney

makes about 8 cups

2 tablespoons vegetable oil

1 tablespoon black mustard seeds

½ teaspoon cardamom seeds

1½ tablespoons cumin seeds

2 medium onions (300g), chopped

2 small red chillies, chopped

5 cloves garlic, crushed

1 tablespoon grated fresh ginger

1½ tablespoons ground coriander

3 teaspoons ground turmeric

6 medium mangoes (2.5kg), peeled, chopped

1 cup (170g) raisins, chopped

1⅓ cups (295g) caster sugar

2 teaspoons salt

1 cup (250ml) white wine vinegar

½ cup (125ml) malt vinegar

Heat oil in large heavy-based pan; cook seeds, stirring, until they pop. Add onions, chillies, garlic and ginger; cook, stirring, until onions are browned lightly. Add ground spices; cook, stirring, until mixture is fragrant. Add remaining ingredients; simmer, uncovered, about 1¼ hours, stirring occasionally, or until thickened. Pour the chutney into hot sterilised jars, seal while hot.

tomato & aubergine pickle

makes about 2½ cups

1 large aubergine (500g)

1 tablespoon salt

2 tablespoons ghee

1 large onion (200g), chopped

3 cloves garlic, crushed

2 small red chillies, chopped

2 large tomatoes (500g), chopped

2 teaspoons sugar

1 teaspoon garam masala

1 teaspoon ground coriander

½ teaspoon chilli powder

1 tablespoon white vinegar

⅔ cup (160ml) water

Peel aubergine; cut into 1cm slices, sprinkle both sides with half the salt. Cover; stand 20 minutes. Rinse aubergine under cold water; pat dry, then chop aubergine into small pieces. Heat ghee in large pan; cook onion, garlic and chillies, stirring, until onion is browned lightly. Add aubergine; cook, stirring, 2 minutes. Add remaining salt, tomatoes, sugar, spices, vinegar and water; cook, stirring occasionally, about 15 minutes or until the mixture has thickened. Cool.

fish & seafood

4 x 220g salmon fillets, skin-on

nam jim

3 long green chillies, chopped

2 fresh small red thai chillies, chopped

2 cloves garlic, quartered

1 shallot (25g), quartered

2cm piece fresh ginger (10g), quartered

⅓ cup (80ml) lime juice

2 tablespoons fish sauce

1 tablespoon grated palm sugar

1 tablespoon groundnut oil

¼ cup (35g) roasted unsalted cashews, chopped finely

herb salad

1½ cups loosely packed fresh mint leaves

1 cup loosely packed coriander leaves

1 cup loosely packed basil leaves, torn

1 medium red onion (170g), sliced thinly

1 cucumber (260g), sliced thinly

grilled salmon with nam jim & herb salad

preparation time 30 minutes ■ cooking time 10 minutes ■ serves 4

1 Make nam jim.

2 Cook salmon, both sides, on heated oiled grill plate (or grill or barbecue) until cooked as desired.

3 Meanwhile, combine ingredients for herb salad in medium bowl.

4 Serve salmon and herb salad topped with nam jim.

■ **nam jim** Blend or process chillies, garlic, shallot, ginger, juice, sauce, sugar and oil until smooth; stir in nuts.

Nam jim is a generic term for a Thai dipping sauce; most versions include fish sauce and chillies, but the remaining ingredients are up to the cook's discretion.

lemongrass fish with daikon salad

preparation time 10 minutes ■ cooking time 20 minutes ■ serves 4

4 small whole snapper (1.5kg)

1 medium brown onion (150g), chopped coarsely

1 clove garlic, quartered

2cm piece fresh ginger (10g), quartered

10cm stick fresh lemongrass (20g), sliced thinly

2 tablespoons tamarind concentrate

1 tablespoon brown sugar

1 tablespoon sambal oelek

1 tablespoon kecap manis

2 teaspoons groundnut oil

½ cup (125ml) water

1 small daikon (400g), cut into matchsticks

1 medium carrot (120g), cut into matchsticks

½ cup loosely packed fresh coriander leaves

1   Preheat oven to 200°C/180°C fan-assisted.

2   Using sharp knife, score each fish three times on each side through thickest part of flesh; place fish in large oiled shallow baking dish.

3   Blend or process onion, garlic, ginger, lemongrass, tamarind, sugar, sambal and kecap manis until mixture forms a smooth paste.

4   Heat oil in small frying pan; cook paste, stirring, 5 minutes. Add the water; bring to a boil. Reduce heat; simmer, uncovered, 2 minutes.

5   Brush half the sauce inside each fish; pour remaining sauce over fish. Roast, uncovered, brushing occasionally, about 15 minutes or until fish is cooked.

6   Meanwhile, combine daikon, carrot and half the coriander in medium bowl.

7   Serve fish sprinkled with remaining coriander, and daikon salad.

prawns dhania masala

preparation time 20 minutes ■ cooking time 8 minutes
■ serves 4 to 6

1.5kg uncooked king prawns
2 tablespoons vegetable oil
1 large onion (200g), sliced

masala paste

⅔ cup firmly packed fresh coriander leaves
⅓ cup firmly packed fresh mint leaves
2 tablespoons water
2 teaspoons sesame oil
2 cloves garlic, chopped
1 tablespoon chopped fresh ginger
2 tablespoons white vinegar
1 teaspoon ground turmeric
1 teaspoon ground cumin
1 teaspoon chilli powder
1 teaspoon ground fennel
½ teaspoon ground cardamom
1 teaspoon salt

1   Shell and devein prawns, leaving tails intact.
2   Blend or process all masala paste ingredients until smooth.
3   Heat oil in large pan; cook onion, stirring, until browned.
4   Add masala paste to pan; cook, stirring, until fragrant. Stir
in prawns; cook 5 minutes or until tender.

garlic & chilli seafood stir-fry

preparation time 25 minutes ■ **cooking time 20 minutes** ■ **serves 4**

720g uncooked medium king prawns

2 cleaned squid hoods (300g)

540g octopus, quartered

¼ cup (60ml) groundnut oil

6 cloves garlic, sliced thinly

2cm piece fresh ginger (10g), sliced thinly

2 fresh long red chillies, sliced thinly

2 tablespoons chinese cooking wine

1 teaspoon caster sugar

4 spring onions, cut in 4cm pieces

chilli fried shallots

1 tablespoon fried shallots

1 teaspoon sea salt flakes

½ teaspoon dried chilli flakes

1 Shell and devein prawns, leaving tails intact. Cut squid down centre to open out; score inside in diagonal pattern then cut into thick strips. Quarter octopus lengthways.

2 Combine ingredients for chilli fried shallots in small bowl.

3 Heat 1 tablespoon of the oil in wok; stir-fry prawns until changed in colour, remove from wok. Heat another tablespoon of the oil in wok; stir-fry squid until cooked through, remove from wok. Heat remaining oil in wok; stir-fry octopus until tender.

4 Stir-fry garlic, ginger and chilli in wok until fragrant. Return seafood to wok with remaining ingredients; stir-fry until hot.

5 Serve stir-fry sprinkled with chilli shallots.

6 fresh small red thai chillies, chopped coarsely
2 cloves garlic, quartered
10 shallots (250g), chopped coarsely
10cm stick fresh lemongrass (20g), chopped coarsely
5cm piece fresh galangal (25g), quartered
¼ cup coarsely chopped coriander root and stem mixture
¼ teaspoon ground turmeric
1 tablespoon groundnut oil
2 x 400ml cans coconut milk
2 tablespoons fish sauce
4 fresh kaffir lime leaves, shredded
1 tablespoon lime juice
4 x 200g white fish fillets
½ cup loosely packed fresh coriander leaves

fish curry in lime & coconut

preparation time 25 minutes ■ cooking time 35 minutes ■ serves 4

1   Blend or process chilli, garlic, shallot, lemongrass, galangal, coriander root and stem mixture, turmeric and oil until mixture forms a smooth paste.

2   Cook paste in large frying pan, stirring, over medium heat, about 3 minutes or until fragrant. Add coconut milk, sauce and lime leaves; bring to a boil. Reduce heat; simmer, uncovered, about 15 minutes or until thickened slightly. Stir in juice.

3   Add fish to pan; simmer, uncovered, about 10 minutes or until cooked. Serve curry sprinkled with coriander leaves.

tip   Use any firm white fish with a meaty texture. Goes well with steamed basmati rice.

goan fish curry

preparation time 25 minutes ■ cooking time 20 minutes
■ serves 4 to 6

½ cup (35g) shredded
coconut, toasted
2 cloves garlic, chopped
3 small red chillies, chopped
2 teaspoons coriander seeds
2 teaspoons cumin seeds
½ teaspoon ground turmeric
1 tablespoon tamarind
concentrate
1 tablespoon finely grated
fresh ginger
2 medium onions (300g),
chopped

½ cup (125ml) cold water
2 tablespoons vegetable oil
2 medium tomatoes (380g),
chopped
8 curry leaves
½ cup (125ml) chicken stock
⅔ cup (85g) coconut milk
powder
⅔ cup (160ml) boiling water
1kg boneless white fish fillets,
chopped

1   Blend or process coconut, garlic, chillies, seeds, turmeric,
tamarind, ginger and half the onions with the cold water until
pureed.
2   Heat oil in large saucepan; cook the remaining onion,
stirring, until browned lightly. Add the coconut mixture; cook,
stirring, until fragrant.
3   Add tomatoes, curry leaves and stock to pan with blended
coconut milk powder and boiling water; simmer, uncovered,
10 minutes or until sauce is thickened.
4   Add fish; simmer, covered, 10 minutes or until fish is tender.

fish fillets
with grilled corn salad

preparation time 15 minutes ■ cooking time 20 minutes
■ serves 4

4 x 200g firm white fish fillets
1 tablespoon soy sauce

grilled corn salad
2 corn cobs (500g), silk and husks removed
250g cherry tomatoes, halved
1 small red onion (100g), sliced thinly
1 small red thai chilli, deseeded, sliced thinly
2 medium avocados (500g), chopped coarsely
¼ cup coarsely chopped fresh coriander
⅓ cup (80ml) lime juice
1 clove garlic, crushed
1 tablespoon olive oil

1   Make grilled corn salad.
2   Brush fish with sauce; cook on heated lightly oiled grill
plate (or grill or barbecue) until cooked as desired. Serve fish
with salad.

■ **grilled corn salad** Cook corn on heated oiled grill plate
(or grill or barbecue) until browned and just tender; cool
10 minutes. Using sharp knife, remove kernels from cob;
combine in medium bowl with remaining ingredients.

chipotle prawns with grilled pineapple, red onion & coriander salad

preparation time 20 minutes ■ **cooking time 30 minutes** ■ **serves 4**

1kg uncooked medium king prawns

2 medium red onions (340g), cut into wedges

1 small pineapple (800g), chopped coarsely

½ cup firmly packed fresh coriander leaves

chipotle paste

3 chipotle chillies

2 tablespoons cider vinegar

2 tablespoons water

1 small brown onion (80g), chopped coarsely

2 cloves garlic, quartered

2 teaspoons ground cumin

1   Make chipotle paste.

2   Shell and devein prawns, leaving tails intact. Combine prawns in medium bowl with half of chipotle paste.

3   Cook onion and pineapple on heated oiled grill plate (or grill or barbecue), uncovered, about 10 minutes or until just tender.

4   Cook prawns on heated oiled grill plate (or grill or barbecue), uncovered, until changed in colour.

5   Combine onion and pineapple in medium bowl with coriander; serve with prawns and remaining chipotle paste.

■ **chipotle paste** Soak chillies in vinegar in small bowl for 10 minutes. Blend or process chilli mixture, the water, onion, garlic and cumin until smooth. Place chipotle paste in small saucepan. Bring to a boil then reduce heat; simmer, uncovered, about 10 minutes or until paste thickens.

meat

twice-fried sichuan beef with pak choy

½ cup (75g) cornflour

1 tablespoon sichuan peppercorns, crushed coarsely

600g piece beef eye fillet, sliced thinly

vegetable oil, for deep-frying

2 teaspoons sesame oil

1 clove garlic, crushed

2 fresh small red thai chillies, chopped finely

1 medium brown onion (150g), sliced thinly

1 medium carrot (120g), halved, sliced thinly

1 medium red pepper (200g), sliced thinly

150g sugar snap peas, trimmed

300g baby pak choy, leaves separated

2 tablespoons oyster sauce

¼ cup (60ml) japanese soy sauce

¼ cup (60ml) beef stock

2 tablespoons dry sherry

1 tablespoon brown sugar

preparation time 20 minutes ■ **cooking time 25 minutes** ■ **serves 4**

1   Combine cornflour and half the peppercorns in medium bowl with beef.

2   Heat vegetable oil in wok; deep-fry beef, in batches, until crisp. Drain on absorbent paper.

3   Heat sesame oil in cleaned wok; stir-fry garlic, chilli and onion until onion softens. Add carrot and pepper; stir-fry until vegetables soften.

4   Return beef to wok with remaining ingredients; stir-fry until pak choy is wilted.

tip Goes well with steamed jasmine rice.

chilli-garlic mince with green beans

preparation time 10 minutes ■ cooking time 15 minutes ■ serves 4

2 cloves garlic, quartered

2 long green chillies, chopped coarsely

2 fresh small red thai chillies, chopped coarsely

1 tablespoon groundnut oil

600g minced beef

150g green beans, chopped coarsely

1 medium red pepper (200g), sliced thinly

2 tablespoons kecap asin

¼ cup (60ml) hoisin sauce

4 spring onions, sliced thickly

2 tablespoons crushed peanuts

1   Blend or process garlic and chilli until mixture is finely chopped.

2   Heat half the oil in wok; stir-fry garlic mixture until fragrant. Add beef; stir-fry, in batches, until cooked through.

3   Heat remaining oil in cleaned wok; stir-fry beans and pepper until tender.

4   Return beef to wok with sauces and onion; stir-fry until hot. Sprinkle over nuts; serve with lime wedges, if you like.

beef dhansak

preparation time 25 minutes ■ cooking time 2 hours
■ serves 6

2 tablespoons ghee
2 medium onions (300g), chopped
4 cloves garlic, crushed
1 teaspoon ground turmeric
2 teaspoons ground coriander
2 teaspoons ground cumin
2 teaspoons garam masala
500g butternut squash, peeled, chopped
1 medium aubergine (300g), peeled, chopped
6 curry leaves
1 cup (200g) masoor dhal (red lentils), rinsed, drained
1 litre (4 cups) water
1kg diced beef

1   Heat ghee in large saucepan; cook onions and garlic, stirring, until browned lightly. Add all the spices; cook, stirring, until fragrant.

2   Add squash to pan along with aubergine, curry leaves, dhal and water; bring to the boil, then immediately simmer. Cook, covered, 30 minutes or until squash is tender. Cool.

3   Blend or process mixture, in batches, until pureed; return to same pan. Add diced beef to pan; bring to the boil, then immediately simmer. Cook, covered, 1 hour. Simmer, uncovered, 30 minutes or until beef is tender and mixture thickened.

beef kofta with aubergine & tomato masala

preparation time 20 minutes (plus refrigeration time) ■ cooking time 45 minutes ■ serves 6 to 8

1 Combine mince, mint, ginger, ground coriander, garam masala, chilli powder and yogurt in medium bowl. Mould tablespoons of mince mixture into oval kofta shapes, place on tray; cover, refrigerate 1 hour.

2 Heat half the ghee in large frying pan; cook kofta, in batches, until browned all over. Drain on absorbent paper.

3 Heat remaining ghee in same pan; cook onions, garlic, cardamom, extra garam masala, turmeric and cumin, stirring, until onions are browned lightly.

4 Add tomatoes, paste, aubergines and chillies; cook, stirring, 5 minutes or until vegetables are soft.

5 Add stock and kofta; simmer, covered, 20 minutes. Simmer, uncovered, 10 minutes or until kofta are cooked through and sauce is thickened. Just before serving, stir in chopped fresh coriander.

750g minced beef
2 tablespoons chopped fresh mint
2 teaspoons finely grated fresh ginger
1 teaspoon ground coriander
½ teaspoon garam masala
1 teaspoon chilli powder
¼ cup (60ml) natural yogurt
3 tablespoons ghee
2 medium onions (300g), sliced
2 cloves garlic, crushed
½ teaspoon ground cardamom
1 teaspoon garam masala, extra
1 teaspoon ground turmeric
1 teaspoon cumin seeds
2 medium tomatoes (380g), chopped
1 tablespoon tomato paste
2 baby aubergines (120g), chopped
2 small red chillies, chopped finely
1 cup (250ml) beef stock
1 tablespoon chopped fresh coriander

1 cup (90g) grated fresh coconut

400g can tomatoes

2 tablespoons grated fresh ginger

2 teaspoons black mustard seeds

1 tablespoon tamarind concentrate

2 tablespoons vegetable oil

2 large onions (400g), sliced

6 cloves garlic, crushed

1 tablespoon ground cumin

1 teaspoon ground turmeric

2 teaspoons ground coriander

2 teaspoons hot chilli powder

2 teaspoons sweet paprika

10 curry leaves

1kg diced beef chuck steak

½ cup (125ml) water

beef madras

preparation time 20 minutes ■ **cooking time 1 hour 30 minutes** ■ **serves 6**

1   Blend or process coconut, undrained tomatoes, ginger, seeds and tamarind until pureed.

2   Heat oil in large saucepan; cook onions and garlic, stirring, until browned lightly. Add all the spices; cook, stirring, until fragrant.

3   Add curry leaves, beef, water and pureed coconut mixture; simmer, covered, 1½ hours, stirring occasionally, or until beef is tender.

punjabi lamb shanks in spinach & tomatoes

preparation time 20 minutes (plus refrigeration time) ■ cooking time 1 hour 45 minutes ■ serves 4

4 cloves garlic

4 large green chillies

1 tablespoon grated fresh ginger

1 tablespoon ground cumin

2 tablespoons vegetable oil

8 trimmed lamb shanks (1.5kg)

2 tablespoons ghee

2 medium onions (300g), sliced

2 bay leaves

4 cloves

1 cinnamon stick

1 cardamom pod, bruised

2 teaspoons garam masala

1 teaspoon ground nutmeg

1 teaspoon ground coriander

1 teaspoon ground cumin, extra

500g spinach, chopped

400g can tomatoes

¼ cup (60ml) tomato paste

1 Blend or process garlic, chillies, ginger, cumin and oil until pureed. Spread chilli mixture all over lamb shanks; cover, refrigerate 3 hours or overnight.

2 Heat ghee in large saucepan; cook onions, stirring, until browned lightly. Add bay leaves and spices; cook, stirring, until fragrant. Add lamb mixture; cook, stirring, until lamb is just browned.

3 Boil, steam or microwave spinach until just wilted; drain. Blend or process spinach, undrained crushed tomatoes and paste until pureed; add to lamb mixture. Simmer, covered, for 1¼ hours. Simmer, uncovered, 30 minutes or until lamb is tender and sauce is thickened.

lamb and macadamia curry

preparation time 20 minutes ■ cooking time 2 hours 20 minutes ■ serves 4

1 cup (140g) roasted unsalted
macadamias
2 tablespoons vegetable oil
800g diced lamb shoulder
1 medium brown onion (150g),
chopped coarsely
1 clove garlic, crushed
2 fresh small red thai chillies,
chopped finely
2cm piece fresh ginger (10g), grated
1 teaspoon ground cumin
1 teaspoon ground turmeric
½ teaspoon ground cinnamon
½ teaspoon ground cardamom
½ teaspoon ground fennel
400g can diced tomatoes
400ml can coconut milk
1 cup (250ml) beef stock
½ cup loosely packed coriander leaves

1 Blend or process half the nuts until finely ground; coarsely chop remaining nuts.
2 Heat half the oil in large saucepan; cook lamb, in batches, until browned.
3 Heat remaining oil in same pan; cook onion, garlic, chilli and ginger, stirring, until onion softens. Add spices; cook, stirring, until fragrant. Return lamb to pan with ground nuts, undrained tomatoes, coconut milk and stock; bring to a boil. Reduce heat; simmer, covered, about 1¼ hours or until lamb is tender. Uncover; simmer about 15 minutes or until sauce thickens slightly.
4 Serve lamb sprinkled with remaining nuts and coriander.

tip Goes well with steamed basmati rice.

1 tablespoon vegetable oil

8 trimmed lamb shanks (2kg)

2 large brown onions (400g), chopped coarsely

400ml can coconut milk

2 tablespoons tamarind concentrate

2 cups (500ml) beef stock

700g butternut squash peeled, cut into 2cm cubes

¼ cup (35g) roasted unsalted peanuts, chopped coarsely

2 spring onions, sliced thinly

massaman curry paste

20 dried red chillies

1 teaspoon ground coriander

2 teaspoons ground cumin

2 teaspoons ground cinnamon

½ teaspoon ground cardamom

½ teaspoon ground clove

5 cloves garlic, quartered

1 large brown onion (200g), chopped coarsely

2 x 10cm sticks fresh lemongrass (40g), sliced thinly

3 fresh kaffir lime leaves, sliced thinly

4cm piece fresh ginger (20g), chopped coarsely

2 teaspoons shrimp paste

1 tablespoon groundnut oil

Having a spicy flavour reminiscent of many Indian or Pakistani dishes, Thai massaman curries evolved from foods originally introduced by Muslim traders from India and Pakistan. Massaman paste remains a favourite of the Muslim communities in southern Thailand for use in hot and sour stew-like curries and sauces.

lamb shanks massaman

preparation time 30 minutes ■ cooking time 2 hours 30 minutes ■ serves 4

1 Preheat oven to 180°C/160°C fan-assisted.

2 Make massaman curry paste.

3 Heat half the oil in large flameproof dish; cook lamb, in batches, until browned.

4 Heat remaining oil in same dish; cook brown onion and ½ cup curry paste, stirring, 2 minutes. Add coconut milk, tamarind and stock; bring to a boil. Remove from heat, add lamb; cook in oven, covered, 2 hours. Remove lamb from dish; cover.

5 Add squash to dish; bring to a boil. Reduce heat; simmer, uncovered, about 10 minutes or until squash is tender and sauce is thickened.

6 Divide lamb, squash and sauce among serving plates, sprinkle with nuts and spring onion.

■ massaman curry paste Place chillies in small heatproof jug, cover with boiling water, stand 15 minutes; drain, reserve chillies. Meanwhile, dry-fry coriander, cumin, cinnamon, cardamom and clove in small frying pan, stirring, until fragrant. Place chillies and roasted spices in small shallow baking dish with remaining ingredients. Roast, uncovered, in oven 15 minutes. Blend or process roasted mixture until smooth. Freeze the remaining curry paste, covered, after you use the ½ cup called for in this recipe.

lamb do piaza

preparation time 20 minutes ■ cooking time 2 hours ■ serves 6 to 8

4 large onions (800g)

3 tablespoons ghee

5 cloves garlic, crushed

1 tablespoon grated fresh ginger

½ teaspoon chilli powder

½ teaspoon ground coriander

1 tablespoon ground cumin

1 teaspoon ground turmeric

½ teaspoon cardamom seeds

4 cloves

1.2kg diced lamb

1 cup (250ml) natural yogurt

400g can tomatoes

2 tablespoons chopped fresh coriander

2 tablespoons chopped fresh mint

1½ teaspoons garam masala

1 Finely slice half the onions. Heat half the ghee in large saucepan; cook sliced onions until browned lightly. Remove from pan; reserve.

2 Finely chop remaining onions. Heat remaining ghee in same pan, add onions, garlic and ginger; cook, stirring, until onions are browned lightly. Stir in chilli powder and all spices; cook, stirring, until fragrant.

3 Stir lamb into spice mixture; add yogurt gradually, in six batches, stirring well between additions.

4 Add undrained crushed tomatoes; simmer, covered, 1½ hours. Remove cover; simmer 30 minutes or until lamb is tender.

5 Just before serving, add reserved onions, herbs and garam masala; stir until heated through.

rogan josh

preparation time 20 minutes (plus refrigeration time) ■ **cooking time 2 hours** ■ **serves 6 to 8**

1 Combine yogurt, vinegar, half the garlic and half the ginger in large bowl, add lamb; toss lamb to coat in marinade. Cover; refrigerate 3 hours or overnight.

2 Heat ghee in large saucepan, add whole spices; cook, stirring, until fragrant. Add onions and remaining garlic and ginger; cook, stirring, until onions are browned lightly.

3 Add ground spices to pan; cook, stirring, until fragrant. Add lamb mixture, stir to coat in spice mixture.

4 Pour stock into pan; simmer, covered, 1½ hours. Simmer, uncovered, 30 minutes or until lamb is tender. Just before serving, stir in garam masala and fresh herbs.

1 cup (250ml) natural yogurt

1 tablespoon malt vinegar

4 cloves garlic, crushed

1 tablespoon grated fresh ginger

1kg diced lamb

2 tablespoons ghee

4 cardamom pods, bruised

3 cloves

1 cinnamon stick

2 medium onions (300g), chopped finely

3 teaspoons ground cumin

1 tablespoon ground coriander

1 teaspoon ground fennel

1½ teaspoons sweet paprika

¾ teaspoon chilli powder

½ cup (125ml) chicken stock

1 teaspoon garam masala

2 tablespoons chopped fresh coriander

1 tablespoon chopped fresh mint

½ cup (40g) desiccated coconut

⅓ cup (80ml) hot water

¼ cup (40g) unsalted roasted cashews

500g minced lamb

1 large brown onion (200g), chopped finely

½ cup (35g) stale breadcrumbs

1 egg

2 tablespoons ghee

2 bay leaves

1 cinnamon stick

5 cardamom pods, bruised

5 cloves

1 medium red onion (170g), sliced thinly

2cm piece fresh ginger (10g), grated

2 cloves garlic, crushed

½ teaspoon chilli powder

½ teaspoon ground turmeric

1 teaspoon ground coriander

½ teaspoon ground cumin

2 medium tomatoes (300g), chopped coarsely

1½ cups (375ml) water, extra

¾ cup (180ml) cream

lamb meatball korma

preparation time 45 minutes (plus standing time) ■ cooking time 1 hour 10 minutes ■ serves 4

1 Place coconut in small heatproof bowl, cover with the hot water; stand 1 hour, drain. Blend or process coconut and nuts until mixture forms a thick puree.

2 Mix 2 tablespoons of the coconut mixture, lamb, brown onion, breadcrumbs and egg in medium bowl; roll level tablespoons of mixture into balls.

3 Melt half the ghee in large saucepan; cook meatballs, in batches, until browned lightly. Drain on absorbent paper.

4 Heat remaining ghee in same cleaned pan; add leaves, cinnamon, cardamom and cloves. Cook, stirring, until fragrant. Add red onion; cook, stirring, until browned lightly. Add ginger, garlic, chilli, turmeric, coriander and cumin; cook, stirring, 1 minute. Add tomato; cook, stirring, about 5 minutes or until mixture thickens slightly. Add remaining coconut mixture and extra water; simmer, uncovered, 20 minutes.

5 Return meatballs to pan; simmer, covered, about 20 minutes or until cooked through. Stir in cream; simmer, stirring, until hot.

tip Goes well with steamed basmati rice.

pork vindaloo

preparation time 20 minutes (plus refrigeration time)
■ **cooking time 1 hour 10 minutes** ■ **serves 6 to 8**

2 teaspoons cumin seeds

2 teaspoons garam masala

1 tablespoon grated fresh
ginger

6 cloves garlic, crushed

8 small red chillies, chopped
finely

1 tablespoon white vinegar

1 tablespoon tamarind
concentrate

1kg diced pork

2 tablespoons ghee

2 large onions (400g),
chopped

2 cinnamon sticks

6 cloves

2 teaspoons plain flour

1 litre (4 cups) beef stock

8 curry leaves

25g jaggery

1   Cook cumin and garam masala in large dry saucepan,
stirring, until fragrant.

2   Combine cooled spice mixture with ginger, garlic, chillies,
vinegar and tamarind in large bowl, add pork; toss pork to
coat in marinade. Cover; refrigerate 1 hour.

3   Heat ghee in same pan; cook onions, cinnamon and
cloves, stirring, until onions are browned lightly. Add pork
mixture; cook, stirring, 5 minutes or until pork is browned
lightly. Stir in flour.

4   Gradually pour in stock, then stir in leaves; simmer,
covered, 30 minutes. Simmer, uncovered, 30 minutes or until
pork is tender and sauce thickened. Add jaggery; stir until
dissolved.

pork & tamarind curry

preparation time 20 minutes (plus standing time)
■ cooking time 1 hour 10 minutes ■ serves 6

60g dried tamarind, chopped

2 cups (500ml) boiling water

1 large onion (200g), chopped

4 cloves garlic

1 teaspoon finely grated fresh
ginger

2 small green chillies

1 tablespoon chopped
lemongrass

2 tablespoons ghee

5 cloves

2 cinnamon sticks

1 teaspoon ground turmeric

1 tablespoon ground coriander

½ teaspoon ground cardamom

1 teaspoon chilli powder

1kg diced pork

1 tablespoon chopped fresh
coriander

1 Combine tamarind and boiling water in small bowl; stand
30 minutes. Strain tamarind over bowl, pressing to extract all
liquid; discard tamarind. Reserve liquid.

2 Blend or process onion, garlic, ginger, chillies, lemongrass
and 1 tablespoon reserved tamarind liquid until pureed.

3 Heat ghee in large saucepan; cook onion mixture, cloves,
cinnamon and spices, stirring, until onion is soft and mixture
fragrant. Add pork; cook, stirring, until pork is coated in spice
mixture and changes colour.

4 Stir in remaining reserved tamarind liquid; simmer,
covered, 30 minutes. Simmer, uncovered, 30 minutes or until
pork is cooked through and tender. Just before serving, stir in
chopped fresh coriander.

chipotle pork ribs
with chorizo & smoked paprika

preparation time 20 minutes ■ cooking time 2 hours 50 minutes ■ serves 4

4 chipotle chillies

1 cup (250ml) boiling water

1.5kg pork belly ribs

1 tablespoon olive oil

170g chorizo sausage, sliced thinly

2 medium red onions (340g), chopped
coarsely

1 medium red pepper (200g), chopped
coarsely

1 medium green pepper (200g), chopped
coarsely

1 teaspoon smoked paprika

4 cloves garlic, crushed

3 x 400g cans crushed tomatoes

2 medium tomatoes (300g), chopped finely

½ cup finely chopped fresh coriander

2 teaspoons finely grated lime rind

1 clove garlic, crushed, extra

1   Preheat oven to moderately slow (160°C/140°C fan-assisted).

2   Soak chillies in the boiling water in small heatproof bowl for 10 minutes. Discard stalks from chillies; reserve chillies and liquid.

3   Using heavy knife, separate ribs. Heat oil in large deep flameproof baking dish; cook ribs, in batches, until browned all over.

4   Cook chorizo, onion, peppers, paprika and garlic in same dish, stirring, until onion softens. Return ribs to dish with undrained crushed tomatoes, chillies and reserved liquid. Cover; cook in oven about 1 hour. Uncover; cook a further 1½ hours or until ribs are tender.

5   Meanwhile, combine chopped tomato, coriander, rind and extra garlic in small bowl. Cover; refrigerate until required.

6   Top ribs with coriander mixture; serve with salsa and flour tortillas, if desired.

plum & star anise pork spareribs with pear, ginger & chilli salad

preparation time 25 minutes (plus refrigeration time) ■ cooking time
30 minutes ■ serves 4

2kg slabs american-style pork spareribs

plum & star anise marinade
1 cup (250ml) ready-made plum sauce
5cm piece fresh ginger (25g), grated
⅓ cup (80ml) oyster sauce
2 star anise
1 teaspoon dried chilli flakes

pear, ginger & chilli salad
2 medium pears (460g), sliced thinly
2 fresh long red chillies, sliced thinly
2 spring onions, sliced thinly
2 cups coarsely chopped fresh mint
2cm piece fresh ginger (10g), grated
2 tablespoons lime juice

1 Make plum and star anise marinade.
2 Place pork in large shallow baking dish; brush marinade all over pork. Pour remaining marinade over pork, cover; refrigerate 3 hours or overnight, turning pork occasionally.
3 Drain pork; reserve marinade. Cook pork on heated oiled grill plate (or grill or barbecue) about 30 minutes or until cooked through, turning and brushing frequently with some of the reserved marinade.
4 Meanwhile, make pear, ginger and chilli salad.
5 Boil remaining marinade, uncovered, in small saucepan about 5 minutes or until thickened slightly.
6 Slice slabs into portions; serve with hot marinade and salad.

■ plum & star anise marinade Combine ingredients in medium saucepan; bring to a boil. Remove from heat; cool 10 minutes.

■ pear, ginger & chilli salad Combine ingredients in medium bowl.

poultry

shantung chicken

preparation time 10 minutes (plus refrigeration time) ■ cooking time
1 hour 20 minutes ■ serves 4

1 clove garlic, crushed

2cm piece fresh ginger (10g), grated

1 tablespoon dark soy sauce

1 tablespoon dry sherry

2 teaspoons sichuan peppercorns, crushed

2 teaspoons groundnut oil

1.6kg whole chicken

shantung sauce

⅓ cup (75g) caster sugar

½ cup (125ml) water

2 tablespoons white wine vinegar

1 fresh small red thai chilli, chopped finely

1 Combine garlic, ginger, sauce, sherry, pepper and oil in large bowl; add chicken, coat in marinade. Cover; refrigerate overnight.

2 Preheat oven to 220°C/200°C fan-assisted.

3 Half-fill a large baking dish with water; place chicken on oiled wire rack set over dish. Roast, uncovered, about 1 hour 20 minutes or until cooked through.

4 Meanwhile, make shantung sauce.

5 Remove chicken from oven; when cool enough to handle, remove bones. Chop meat coarsely; serve drizzled with sauce.

shantung sauce Combine sugar and the water in small saucepan; stir over low heat until sugar dissolves. Bring to a boil; boil, uncovered, without stirring, about 5 minutes or until sauce thickens slightly. Remove from heat; stir in vinegar and chilli.

tip Goes well with crisp fried noodles.

Japanese dry rice wine, sake, is also a basic ingredient in many of the country's most well-known dishes. Special and first-grade sake is sold for drinking while ryoriyo sake, with its lower alcohol content, is made especially for use in marinades, cooking and dipping sauces.

800g chicken breast fillets
½ cup (125ml) cooking sake
1 clove garlic, crushed
1 fresh long red chilli, chopped finely
2 tablespoons rice vinegar
2 tablespoons japanese soy sauce
1 tablespoon lemon juice
2 teaspoons sesame oil
1 teaspoon caster sugar
2 spring onions, sliced thinly
2 tablespoons pickled ginger, shredded finely

sake chicken

preparation time 10 minutes ■ cooking time 15 minutes ■ serves 4

1 Combine chicken, sake, garlic, chilli, vinegar, sauce, juice, oil and sugar in large frying pan; bring to a boil. Reduce heat; simmer, covered, about 10 minutes or until chicken is cooked through. Remove from heat; stand chicken in poaching liquid for 10 minutes before slicing thickly. Cover to keep warm.

2 Bring poaching liquid to a boil; boil, uncovered, about 5 minutes or until sauce thickens. Serve chicken drizzled with sauce, topped with onion and ginger.

tip Goes well with steamed koshihikari rice.

spicy tamarind chicken

preparation time 10 minutes ■ cooking time 1 hour ■ serves 4

4 chicken leg joints (1.5kg)

1 cup (250ml) water

¼ cup (85g) tamarind concentrate

¼ cup (60ml) japanese soy sauce

⅓ cup (90g) firmly packed grated palm sugar

chilli, ginger & lime paste

2 fresh small red thai chillies

5cm piece fresh ginger (25g), chopped coarsely

6 shallots (150g), chopped coarsely

2 cloves garlic

3 fresh kaffir lime leaves

1 tablespoon vegetable oil

1 tablespoon water

1 Make chilli, ginger and lime paste.

2 Preheat oven to 180°C/160°C fan-assisted.

3 Heat oiled large shallow flameproof dish; cook chicken, uncovered, until browned, turning occasionally.

4 Remove chicken from dish. Cook paste, stirring, in same heated dish until fragrant. Stir in remaining ingredients then return chicken to dish, turning to coat in paste mixture.

5 Cook chicken, uncovered, in oven about 30 minutes or until cooked through, brushing frequently with paste mixture. Serve with lime wedges, if you like.

■ **chilli, ginger and lime paste** Blend or process ingredients until mixture forms a smooth paste.

tip Goes well with thin rice noodles.

800g chicken thigh fillets, sliced thinly

¼ cup (60ml) fish sauce

1 tablespoon grated palm sugar

¼ teaspoon ground white pepper

1 tablespoon groundnut oil

3 cloves garlic, sliced thinly

2cm piece fresh ginger (10g), sliced thinly

½ teaspoon dried chilli flakes

250g green beans, cut into 5cm lengths

2 medium yellow peppers (400g), sliced thinly

⅓ cup (80ml) chinese cooking wine

⅓ cup (80ml) lemon juice

1 tablespoon dark soy sauce

½ cup loosely packed thai basil leaves

thai basil chicken & green bean stir-fry

preparation time 20 minutes (plus refrigeration time) ■ cooking time 20 minutes ■ serves 4

1 Combine chicken, fish sauce, sugar and pepper in large bowl, cover; refrigerate 1 hour.

2 Heat oil in wok; stir-fry chicken mixture about 10 minutes or until almost cooked. Add garlic, ginger, chilli, beans and peppers; stir-fry until beans are tender.

3 Add wine, juice and soy sauce; bring to a boil. Reduce heat; simmer, uncovered, 2 minutes. Remove from heat; stir in basil.

tip Goes well with fresh wide rice noodles.

grilled chicken with coriander & chilli

preparation time 10 minutes (plus refrigeration time) ■ cooking time
25 minutes ■ serves 4

8 chicken thigh cutlets (1.6kg)

coriander & chilli paste
2 teaspoons coriander seeds
4 fresh small red thai chillies, chopped
coarsely
1 teaspoon ground cumin
2 whole cloves
2 cardamom pods, bruised
¼ teaspoon ground turmeric
10cm stick fresh lemongrass (20g),
chopped coarsely
2 medium brown onions (300g),
chopped coarsely
4 cloves garlic
⅓ cup (80ml) lime juice
2 teaspoons coarse cooking salt
2 tablespoons groundnut oil

1   Make coriander and chilli paste.
2   Pierce chicken all over with sharp knife. Combine paste and chicken in large
bowl, rubbing paste into cuts. Cover; refrigerate overnight.
3   Cook chicken, covered, on heated oiled grill plate (or grill or barbecue),
5 minutes. Uncover; cook, turning occasionally, about 20 minutes or until cooked.
Serve with lime wedges, if you like.

■ **coriander and chilli paste**   Blend or process ingredients until mixture forms
a smooth paste.

tip Goes well with thin rice noodles.

2 small mandarins (200g)

½ cup (135g) firmly packed grated palm sugar

½ cup (125ml) water

⅓ cup (80ml) mandarin juice

1 tablespoon lime juice

2 teaspoons fish sauce

1 fresh long red chilli, chopped finely

1 star anise

2 tablespoons plain flour

2 teaspoons sea salt flakes

1 teaspoon dried chilli flakes

4 duck breast fillets (600g)

4 spring onions, sliced thinly

½ cup loosely packed fresh mint leaves

1 fresh long red chilli, sliced thinly

tip You need about six small mandarins in total for this recipe: two for the rind and segments, and four for the required amount of juice.

crisp duck with mandarin, chilli & mint

preparation time 25 minutes ■ cooking time 30 minutes ■ serves 4

1 Using vegetable peeler, cut four 5cm-strips of peel from mandarins. Remove remaining peel and pith; discard. Segment mandarins into small heatproof bowl.

2 Combine peel, sugar and the water in small saucepan. Stir over low heat until sugar dissolves; bring to a boil. Reduce heat; simmer, uncovered, without stirring, about 10 minutes or until syrup thickens slightly. Add juices, sauce, chopped chilli and star anise to pan; bring to a boil. Reduce heat; simmer, uncovered, about 5 minutes or until thickened slightly. Discard star anise; pour dressing into bowl with mandarin segments. Cool.

3 Meanwhile, combine flour, salt and dried chilli in medium bowl. Coat duck fillets, one at a time, in flour mixture; shake off excess. Cook duck, skin-side down, in heated oiled large frying pan, over medium heat, about 10 minutes or until crisp. Turn duck; cook about 5 minutes or until cooked as desired. Remove from heat; slice thickly.

4 Divide duck and mandarin segments among serving plates; top with onion, mint and sliced chilli, drizzle with dressing.

pistachio chicken

1kg chicken thigh fillets, cut into 3cm
pieces
1⅓ cups (400g) natural yogurt
2 teaspoons groundnut oil
¼ cup coarsely chopped fresh coriander
¼ cup (35g) coarsely chopped roasted
unsalted pistachios

pistachio paste

¾ cup (105g) roasted unsalted pistachios
1 medium brown onion (150g), chopped
coarsely
⅓ cup (95g) yogurt
2 tablespoons groundnut oil
2 cloves garlic, quartered
1 long green chilli, chopped coarsely
1 tablespoon lemon juice
1 teaspoon ground coriander
1 teaspoon ground cumin
½ teaspoon ground cardamom

preparation time 15 minutes (plus refrigeration time) ■ **cooking time 30
minutes** ■ **serves 4**

1 Make pistachio paste.
2 Combine chicken, yogurt and ½ cup of the paste in medium bowl, cover;
refrigerate 30 minutes.
3 Heat oil in large saucepan; cook remaining paste, stirring, until fragrant.
Add chicken mixture; bring to a boil. Reduce heat; simmer, covered, about
20 minutes or until chicken is cooked through.
4 Sprinkle chicken with coriander and nuts.

■ **pistachio paste** Blend or process ingredients until mixture forms
a smooth paste.

tip Goes well with steamed basmati rice. ■ If you can't
buy shelled pistachios, soak shelled nuts in boiling water for
about 5 minutes; drain, then pat dry with absorbent paper.
Rub skins with cloth to peel.

chicken enchiladas

preparation time 50 minutes (plus standing time) ■ cooking time 35 minutes
■ serves 10

3 chipotle chillies

1 cup (250ml) boiling water

500g chicken breast fillets

1 tablespoon vegetable oil

1 large red onion (300g), chopped finely

2 cloves garlic, crushed

1 teaspoon ground cumin

1 tablespoon tomato paste

2 x 425g cans crushed tomatoes

1 tablespoon finely chopped fresh oregano

⅔ cup (160g) soured cream

1½ cups (240g) coarsely grated cheddar

10 small flour tortillas

1 Cover chillies with the water in small heatproof bowl; stand 20 minutes. Remove stems from chillies; discard stems. Blend or process chillies with soaking liquid until smooth.

2 Meanwhile, place chicken in medium saucepan of boiling water. Return to a boil then reduce heat; simmer, covered, about 10 minutes or until chicken is cooked through. Remove chicken from poaching liquid; cool 10 minutes. Discard poaching liquid; shred chicken finely.

3 Preheat oven to moderate (180°C/160°C fan-assisted). Lightly oil shallow rectangular 3-litre (12-cup) ovenproof dish.

4 Heat oil in large frying pan; cook onion, stirring, until softened. Reserve half of onion in small bowl.

5 Add garlic and cumin to remaining onion in pan; cook, stirring, until fragrant. Add chilli mixture, tomato paste, undrained tomatoes and oregano. Bring to a boil then reduce heat; simmer, uncovered, 1 minute. Remove sauce from heat.

6 Meanwhile, combine shredded chicken, reserved onion, half of soured cream and third of cheese in medium bowl.

7 Heat tortillas according to manufacturer's instructions. Dip tortillas, one at a time, in tomato sauce in pan; place on board. Place ¼ cup of chicken mixture along edge of each tortilla; roll enchiladas to enclose filling.

8 Spread ½ cup tomato sauce into prepared dish. Place enchiladas, seam-side down, in dish (they should fit snugly, without overcrowding). Pour remaining tomato sauce over enchiladas; sprinkle with remaining cheese. Cook, uncovered, about 15 minutes or until cheese melts and enchiladas are heated through. Sprinkle with coriander leaves, if desired. Serve with remaining soured cream.

chicken wings with cherry tomato salsa

preparation time 5 minutes (plus refrigeration time) ■ **cooking time 25 minutes** ■ **serves 4**

8 large chicken wings (1kg)

½ teaspoon dried oregano

¼ teaspoon chilli powder

1 teaspoon sweet paprika

½ teaspoon ground cumin

2 tablespoons tomato sauce

1 tablespoon vegetable oil

⅓ cup (80ml) lime juice

500g cherry tomatoes

2 medium avocados (500g), chopped coarsely

310g can corn kernels, drained

1 medium red onion (170g), chopped finely

¼ cup firmly packed fresh coriander leaves

1   Preheat oven to moderately hot (200°C/180°C fan-assisted).

2   Combine chicken, spices, sauce, oil and 1 tablespoon of juice in large bowl; toss to coat chicken in marinade. Refrigerate 2 hours.

3   Place chicken, in single layer, in oiled large shallow baking dish; roast about 25 minutes or until chicken is cooked through.

4   Meanwhile, quarter tomatoes; combine in medium bowl with avocado, corn, onion, coriander and remaining juice.

5   Serve salsa topped with wings.

south indian chicken curry

preparation time 20 minutes ■ cooking time 1 hour
■ serves 4 to 6

2 tablespoons vegetable oil
2 teaspoons black mustard
seeds
¼ teaspoon fenugreek seeds
16 curry leaves, torn
2 large onions (400g),
chopped finely
3 cloves garlic, crushed
1 tablespoon grated fresh
ginger
1 small red chilli, chopped
1 tablespoon ground coriander
2 teaspoons ground sweet
paprika

1 teaspoon ground turmeric
¾ teaspoon ground fennel
1 teaspoon salt
10 chicken thigh cutlets
(1.6kg), skin removed
400g can tomatoes
¼ cup (60ml) chicken stock
300g green beans
1¼ cups (310ml) coconut
cream
1 tablespoon tamarind
concentrate

1   Heat oil in large saucepan; cook seeds and curry leaves,
stirring, until fragrant. Add onions, garlic, ginger and chilli;
cook, stirring, until onions are browned lightly.
2   Add ground spices and salt; cook, stirring, 1 minute.
3   Add chicken to pan along with undrained crushed
tomatoes and stock; simmer, covered, 30 minutes. Remove
lid; simmer 20 minutes or until sauce is thickened slightly.
4   Add beans to pan along with cream and tamarind; simmer,
uncovered, 10 minutes or until beans are tender.

red chicken curry

preparation time 15 minutes ■ cooking time 35 minutes
■ serves 4 to 6

2 tablespoons ghee

2 medium onions (300g),
sliced

4 cloves garlic, crushed

2 teaspoons finely grated
fresh ginger

1 medium red pepper (200g),
chopped

2 teaspoons ground cumin

2 teaspoons ground coriander

2 teaspoons sweet paprika

1 teaspoon hot chilli powder

1 tablespoon tomato paste

425g can tomatoes

9 chicken thigh fillets (1kg)

2 cups (500ml) chicken stock

¼ cup (60ml) cream

1 tablespoon tamarind
concentrate

red food colouring, optional

1   Heat ghee in large saucepan, add onions, garlic, ginger,
pepper and spices; cook, stirring, until onions are browned
lightly.

2   Add paste to pan along with undrained crushed tomatoes,
chicken and stock; simmer, covered, 20 minutes or until
chicken is cooked through.

3   Stir cream, tamarind and food colouring, if using, into
curry. Simmer, uncovered, 15 minutes or until mixture has
thickened slightly.

tamarind, lime & honey chicken salad

preparation time 35 minutes (plus refrigeration time) ■ **cooking time 20 minutes** ■ **serves 4**

1 Combine 1 tablespoon of the oil, tamarind, honey, sauce, rind, juice, garlic and chicken in large bowl, cover; refrigerate 3 hours or overnight.

2 Make honey lime dressing.

3 Heat remaining oil in large frying pan; cook chicken mixture, in batches, until cooked through. Stand 5 minutes; slice chicken thickly. Cover to keep warm.

4 Meanwhile, combine dressing in large bowl with remaining ingredients. Divide salad among plates; top with chicken.

■ **honey lime dressing** Combine ingredients in screw-top jar; shake well.

¼ cup (60ml) groundnut oil

¼ cup (60ml) tamarind concentrate

1 tablespoon honey

2 teaspoons dark soy sauce

½ teaspoon finely grated lime rind

1 tablespoon lime juice

1 clove garlic, crushed

800g chicken breast fillets

½ small chinese cabbage (350g), trimmed, shredded finely

4 spring onions, sliced thinly

500g red radishes, trimmed, sliced thinly, cut into matchsticks

1 cucumber (260g), cut into matchsticks

½ cup loosely packed fresh mint leaves

½ cup loosely packed fresh coriander leaves

⅔ cup (50g) fried shallots

honey lime dressing

1 tablespoon honey

2 tablespoons lime juice

1 teaspoon sesame oil

1 tablespoon dark soy sauce

1 fresh long red chilli, chopped finely

vegetables

spicy carrot & courgette bhajis

1 cup (150g) besan flour

2 teaspoons coarse cooking salt

½ cup (125ml) cold water

¼ teaspoon ground turmeric

1 teaspoon chilli powder

1 teaspoon garam masala

2 cloves garlic, crushed

2 small brown onions (160g), sliced thinly

1 medium carrot (120g), grated coarsely

1 medium courgette (120g),
grated coarsely

½ cup loosely packed fresh
coriander leaves

vegetable oil, for deep-frying

1 cup (320g) mango chutney

preparation time 15 minutes ■ cooking time 15 minutes ■ makes 20

1   Whisk besan flour, salt and the water in medium bowl until mixture forms a smooth thick batter. Stir in spices, garlic, onion, carrot, courgette and coriander.
2   Heat oil in wok; deep-fry tablespoons of mixture, in batches, until vegetables are tender and bhaji are browned lightly. Drain on absorbent paper. Serve with chutney.

The bustling streets of Indian cities are lined with many food stalls that sell a wide array of snacks, one of the most more-ish being bhaji, one or more vegetables grated, dredged in besan (chickpea) flour and deep-fried into fritter-like bites. Grated courgettes can release a lot of water; if bhaji batter becomes runny, add enough besan flour to restore the batter to its original consistency.

sichuan aubergine, almond & chinese cabbage stir-fry

preparation time 15 minutes ■ cooking time 20 minutes
■ serves 4

⅓ cup (55g) blanched almonds, halved

1 tablespoon groudnut oil

1 medium brown onion (150g), chopped coarsely

2 cloves garlic, crushed

1 fresh small red thai chilli, chopped finely

12 baby aubergines (720g), sliced thickly

150g green beans, trimmed, chopped coarsely

1 small chinese cabbage (700g), trimmed, chopped

2 teaspoons sichuan peppercorns, crushed coarsely

¼ cup (60ml) vegetable stock

2 tablespoons hoisin sauce

1 tablespoon dark soy sauce

1 tablespoon red wine vinegar

½ cup loosely packed thai basil leaves

1 fresh long red chilli, sliced thinly

1   Stir-fry nuts in heated wok until browned lightly; remove from wok.

2   Heat oil in wok; stir-fry onion, garlic and thai chilli until onion softens. Add aubergine and beans; stir-fry until tender. Add chinese cabbage; stir-fry until wilted.

3   Add pepper, stock, sauces and vinegar; stir-fry until hot. Remove from heat; stir in basil. Serve sprinkled with nuts and chilli.

spinach & mushroom korma

preparation time 15 minutes ■ cooking time 25 minutes
■ serves 4

⅓ cup (50g) unsalted roasted cashews

1 tablespoon ghee

1 large brown onion (200g), sliced thinly

2 cloves garlic, crushed

4cm piece fresh ginger (20g), grated

2 teaspoons nigella seeds

½ cup (160g) prepared korma paste

⅔ cup (160ml) cream

400g chestnut mushrooms

500g spinach, trimmed, chopped coarsely

⅓ cup (95g) natural yogurt

1   Blend or process nuts until finely ground.

2   Heat ghee in large saucepan; cook onion, garlic and
ginger, stirring, until onion softens. Add nuts, seeds and paste;
cook, stirring, until fragrant.

3   Add cream and mushrooms; simmer, covered, 15 minutes.
Add spinach; cook, stirring, until wilted.

4   Serve curry with yogurt.

In Indian cooking terms, masala literally means ground or blended spices but, informally, has come to mean a 'mix' or 'mixture'; a masala can be whole or ground spices, a paste or powder, or a sauce-like curry incorporating solid elements.

■ Romano peppers, also known as banana chillies or hungarian peppers, are almost as mild as pepper, but have a distinctively sweet sharpness to their taste. Sold in varying degrees of ripeness, they can be found in pale olive green, yellow, orange and red varieties at greengrocers and supermarkets.

■ A popular unleavened Indian bread, similar in appearance to pitta only thinner, chapatis accompany saucy curries, often serving as cutlery to scoop up the food. They are available in the bread department of most supermarkets, delicatessens and Asian food stores.

peppers filled with potato masala

preparation time 20 minutes ■ cooking time 1 hour 20 minutes ■ serves 4

500g potatoes, chopped coarsely
1 tablespoon vegetable oil
1 clove garlic, crushed
1 medium brown onion (150g), sliced thinly
½ teaspoon yellow mustard seeds
1 teaspoon garam masala
1 teaspoon ground coriander
½ teaspoon ground cumin

½ teaspoon chilli powder
¼ teaspoon ground turmeric
400g can chopped tomatoes
2 tablespoons sultanas
4 romano peppers (500g)
½ cucumber, chopped finely
¾ cup (200g) greek-style yogurt
6 chapatis (280g), warmed

1   Preheat oven to 180°C/160°C fan-assisted.

2   Boil, steam or microwave potato until tender; drain. Using fork, crush potato roughly.

3   Heat oil in large frying pan; cook garlic and onion, stirring, until onion softens. Add spices; cook, stirring, until fragrant. Add undrained tomatoes; cook, stirring, 5 minutes. Stir in potato and sultanas.

4   Make lengthways slit in each pepper, stopping 1cm from top and bottom, taking care not to cut all the way through; remove and discard seeds and membranes. Divide potato filling among pepper cavities. Place peppers on oiled oven tray; roast, covered, 30 minutes. Uncover; roast 20 minutes.

5   Make raita by combining cucumber and yogurt in small bowl. Serve peppers with raita and chapatis.

dhal & paneer vegetable curry

2 tablespoons ghee

1 medium brown onion (150g),
chopped finely

2 cloves garlic, crushed

2cm piece fresh ginger (10g), grated

2 teaspoons ground cumin

1 tablespoon ground coriander

1 teaspoon ground turmeric

2 teaspoons garam masala

2 cardamom pods, bruised

2 tablespoons mild curry paste

1 cup (200g) yellow split peas

810g can crushed tomatoes

2 cups (500ml) vegetable stock

2 cups (500ml) water

250g cabbage, chopped coarsely

2 medium carrots (240g), cut into 2cm
pieces

½ cup (60g) frozen peas

2 x 100g packets paneer cheese, cut into
2cm pieces

⅓ cup loosely packed fresh coriander
leaves

preparation time 25 minutes ■ cooking time 1 hour 15 minutes ■ serves 4

1   Heat ghee in large saucepan; cook onion, garlic and ginger, stirring, until onion softens. Add spices; cook, stirring, until fragrant. Add curry paste; cook, stirring, until fragrant.

2   Add split peas, undrained tomatoes, stock and the water; bring to a boil. Reduce heat; simmer, covered, 30 minutes, stirring occasionally. Uncover, add cabbage and carrot; cook, stirring occasionally, about 30 minutes or until split peas soften.

3   Add frozen peas and cheese; cook, uncovered, about 5 minutes or until cheese is heated through. Serve curry sprinkled with coriander.

tip You will need about a quarter of a small cabbage for this recipe.

drunken beans

preparation time 10 minutes (plus standing time)
■ cooking time 1 hour 40 minutes ■ serves 4

1 cup (200g) dried pinto beans
3 bacon rashers (210g), rind removed, chopped coarsely
1 medium brown onion (150g), chopped finely
1 clove garlic, crushed
1 teaspoon ground cumin
½ teaspoon cayenne pepper
1 tablespoon tomato paste
425g can crushed tomatoes
1 cup (250ml) water
1 cup (250ml) beer
1 tablespoon worcestershire sauce
2 tablespoons brown sugar

1   Place beans in medium bowl, cover with water; stand overnight. Drain.

2   Cook bacon, onion, garlic and spices in lightly oiled large saucepan, stirring, until onion softens. Add drained beans and remaining ingredients. Bring to a boil then reduce heat; simmer, covered, about 1½ hours or until beans are just tender.

tomato, olive & radish salad

preparation time 15 minutes (plus refrigeration time)
■ serves 8

1½ cups (180g) pitted black olives
200g baby plum tomatoes
14 medium red radishes (490g), trimmed, quartered
200g button mushrooms, halved
½ cup fresh flat-leaf parsley leaves

moroccan dressing
2 teaspoons moroccan seasoning
½ teaspoon ground coriander
½ teaspoon sweet paprika
2 tablespoons red wine vinegar
⅓ cup (80ml) extra virgin olive oil

1   Combine dressing ingredients in screw-top jar; shake well.
2   Combine salad ingredients in medium bowl with the dressing. Cover; refrigerate at least two hours before serving.

tips Recipe can be prepared a day ahead – add the dressing up to three hours before serving ■ Moroccan seasoning is available from most Middle-Eastern food stores, spice shops and major supermarkets

4 untrimmed corn cobs (1.6kg)

2 teaspoons groundnut oil

2 cloves garlic, crushed

1 small white onion (80g), chopped finely

1 small red pepper (150g), chopped finely

1 fresh long red chilli, chopped finely

1½ cups (300g) white medium-grain rice

1 cup (250ml) vegetable stock

1 cup (250ml) water

chunky salsa

3 medium tomatoes (450g), chopped coarsely

¼ cup (60g) pickled jalapeño chillies

½ cup coarsely chopped fresh coriander

1 clove garlic, crushed

2 tablespoons lime juice

barbecued corn with chunky salsa & mexican rice

preparation time 20 minutes (plus refrigeration time) ■ cooking time 30 minutes ■ serves 4

1　Gently peel husk down corn cob, keeping husk attached at base. Remove as much silk as possible then bring husk back over cob to re-wrap and enclose completely. Place corn in large bowl, add enough cold water to completely submerge corn.

2　Heat oil in medium saucepan; cook garlic, onion, pepper and chilli, stirring, until onion softens. Add rice; cook, stirring, 1 minute. Add stock and the water. Bring to a boil then reduce heat; simmer, covered, about 20 minutes or until rice is just tender. Remove from heat; fluff rice with fork.

3　Meanwhile, drain corn. Cook corn on heated oiled grill plate (or grill or barbecue) about 25 minutes or until corn is tender, turning occasionally.

4　Make chunky salsa.

5　Serve corn with rice and salsa.

■ **chunky salsa** Combine ingredients for chunky salsa in medium bowl.

black bean, corn & chipotle stew

preparation time 15 minutes (plus standing time) ■ cooking time 1 hour
■ serves 4

1½ cups (300g) dried black beans

2 chipotle chillies

½ cup (125ml) boiling water

1 tablespoon cumin seeds

2 trimmed corn cobs (500g)

2 teaspoons olive oil

1 large brown onion (200g), chopped
finely

810g can crushed tomatoes

8 white corn tortillas

onion salsa

1 small red onion (100g), chopped
coarsely

1 small tomato (90g), chopped coarsely

½ cup coarsely chopped fresh coriander

½ cucumber (130g), chopped coarsely

1 tablespoon olive oil

2 tablespoons lemon juice

1   Place beans in medium bowl, cover with water; stand overnight, drain. Rinse under cold water; drain. Place beans in medium saucepan of boiling water. Return to a boil then reduce heat; simmer, uncovered, about 15 minutes or until beans are just tender. Drain.

2   Preheat oven to moderately hot (200°C/180°C fan-assisted).

3   Place chillies and the boiling water in small bowl; stand 15 minutes. Discard stalks; blend or process chilli and soaking liquid until smooth.

4   Meanwhile, dry-fry cumin seeds in small frying pan, stirring, until fragrant.

5   Cook corn on heated oiled grill plate (or grill or barbecue) until browned lightly and just tender. When cool enough to handle, cut kernels from cobs using a sharp knife.

6   Heat oil in large flameproof dish; cook onion, stirring, until softened. Add drained beans, chilli mixture, cumin, undrained tomatoes and half of corn; bring to a boil. Cook in oven about 20 minutes or until sauce thickens.

7   Meanwhile, heat tortillas according to manufacturer's instructions. Make salsa.

8   Serve stew with tortillas and salsa.

■ **salsa** Combine remaining corn with salsa ingredients in medium bowl.

1 cup (200g) toor dhal (yellow split peas)
2 tablespoons vegetable oil
1 large onion (200g), sliced
1 tablespoon ground ginger
2 teaspoons ground cumin
2 teaspoons ground coriander
1 teaspoon ground turmeric
6 cardamom pods, bruised
8 curry leaves
1 teaspoon salt
2 x 400g cans tomatoes
½ cup (35g) shredded coconut
40g jaggery
1 tablespoon tamarind concentrate
1 tablespoon yellow mustard seeds
1kg small new potatoes, halved
500g sweet potatoes, chopped
2 medium carrots (240g), chopped
4 medium courgettes (480g), chopped
½ cup (125ml) water
1 tablespoon lime juice

vegetable and lentil sambar

preparation time 15 minutes (plus soaking time) ■ cooking time 40 minutes ■ serves 6 to 8

1 Put dhal in bowl, cover with water, soak 1 hour; drain.
2 Heat oil in large saucepan; cook onion, stirring, until browned lightly. Add all spices, curry leaves and salt; cook, stirring, until fragrant.
3 Blend or process undrained crushed tomatoes, coconut, jaggery, tamarind and mustard seeds until smooth.
4 Add tomato mixture and dhal to onion mixture; boil, then immediately simmer, covered, 10 minutes.
5 Add potatoes, sweet potatoes and carrots; simmer, covered, 15 minutes. Add remaining ingredients; simmer, covered, 10 minutes or until vegetables are just tender.

bengali crunchy potatoes

preparation time 15 minutes ■ cooking time 25 minutes
■ serves 6

1.5kg potatoes, chopped

1 tablespoon ghee

1 tablespoon panch phora (the Bengali equivalent of
Chinese five-spice)

3 cloves garlic, crushed

1 tablespoon grated fresh ginger

1 small red chilli, chopped

1 tablespoon ground cumin

3 tablespoons ghee, extra

1 teaspoon salt

1 teaspoon cracked black pepper

¼ cup (60ml) lemon juice

¼ cup chopped fresh coriander

1 Boil, steam or microwave potatoes until almost tender; drain.
2 Heat ghee in small frying pan; cook panch phora, stirring,
until fragrant. Add garlic, ginger, chilli and cumin; cook, stirring,
1 minute. Remove from heat.
3 Heat half the extra ghee in large frying pan; add half the
potatoes, stir gently 5 minutes or until browned and crisp.
Remove from pan; repeat with remaining ghee and potatoes.
4 Return potatoes, with spice mixture, salt, pepper and juice,
to pan; stir until just heated through. Just before serving,
sprinkle with fresh coriander.

cauliflower, pea & potato bhaji

preparation time 15 minutes ■ cooking time 30 minutes
■ serves 4 to 6

2 tablespoons ghee

1 large onion (200g), sliced

2 cloves garlic, crushed

1 tablespoon sweet paprika

2 teaspoons garam masala

2 teaspoons ground cumin

6 cardamom pods, bruised

4 cloves

4 medium potatoes (800g), unpeeled, quartered

8 curry leaves

⅓ cup (30g) shredded coconut

½ cup (125ml) water

400ml can coconut milk

2 teaspoons salt

1 small cauliflower (1kg), chopped

1 cup (125g) frozen peas

1   Heat ghee in medium saucepan; cook onion and garlic, stirring, until onion is browned lightly. Add all spices; cook, stirring, until fragrant.

2   Add potatoes, curry leaves, coconut, water, coconut milk and salt; simmer, covered, 15 minutes, until potatoes are just tender.

3   Add cauliflower; simmer, covered, 10 minutes or until cauliflower is just tender. Stir in peas; simmer until peas are heated through.

spicy okra

preparation time 15 minutes ■ cooking time 35 minutes ■ serves 4 to 6

2 tablespoons vegetable oil

2 medium onions (300g), sliced

1 tablespoon cumin seeds

4 cloves garlic, crushed

2 long green chillies, chopped

4 curry leaves

2 teaspoons ground coriander

1 teaspoon ground turmeric

½ teaspoon ground sweet paprika

½ teaspoon ground ginger

1kg okra

1 cup (250ml) water

¼ cup (60ml) tomato paste

2 tablespoons white vinegar

2 teaspoons sugar

¼ cup firmly packed fresh coriander leaves

½ teaspoon garam masala

1   Heat oil in large frying pan; cook onions, stirring, until browned lightly. Add the seeds; cook, stirring, until seeds start to pop. Add garlic, chillies, curry leaves, ground coriander, turmeric, paprika and ginger; cook, stirring, until fragrant.

2   Add okra, stir to coat in the spice mixture. Add water, paste, vinegar and sugar; boil, then immediately simmer, covered, 30 minutes, stirring occasionally, or until okra is tender. Just before serving, stir in fresh coriander and sprinkle with garam masala.

mixed vegetable curry

preparation time 20 minutes (plus standing time) ■ cooking
time 25 minutes ■ serves 4

¼ cup (60ml) natural yogurt

2 cloves garlic, crushed

2 teaspoons grated fresh
ginger

1 teaspoon salt

¼ teaspoon cracked black
pepper

1 teaspoon ground coriander

1 teaspoon chilli powder

½ teaspoon garam masala

4 cardamom pods, bruised

2 medium potatoes (400g)

3 tablespoons ghee

1 tablespoon vegetable oil

2 medium onions (300g),
sliced

1 large carrot (180g), sliced

300g cauliflower florets

2 baby aubergines (120g),
sliced

2 bay leaves

½ cup (125ml) water

1 cup (250ml) coconut cream

150g green beans, halved

2 tablespoons chopped fresh
mint

1 Combine yogurt, garlic, ginger, salt, pepper and spices in small
bowl; stand 15 minutes. Roughly chop potatoes.

2 Heat ghee and oil together in large saucepan; cook onions,
stirring, until onions are browned lightly. Add potatoes, carrot,
cauliflower, aubergines and bay leaves; cook, stirring, 5 minutes.

3 Add yogurt mixture, water and coconut cream; simmer, covered,
15 minutes or until potatoes are just tender.

4 Add beans; simmer, uncovered, further 5 minutes or until beans
are just tender. Just before serving, sprinkle with chopped mint.

rice & noodles

nasi goreng

preparation time 25 minutes ■ cooking time 15 minutes ■ serves 4

Nasi goreng, which translates simply as 'fried rice' in Indonesia and Malaysia, was first created to use up yesterday's leftovers. You need to cook 2 cups (400g) white long-grain rice the day before making this recipe. Spread it in a thin layer on a tray and refrigerate it overnight. Dried chinese sausages, also called lop chong, are usually made from pork and sold, strung together, in Asian food stores.

720g cooked medium king prawns
1 tablespoon groundnut oil
175g dried chinese sausages, sliced thickly
1 medium brown onion (150g), sliced thinly
1 medium red pepper (200g), sliced thinly
2 fresh long red chillies, sliced thinly
2 cloves garlic, crushed

2cm piece fresh ginger (10g), grated
1 teaspoon shrimp paste
4 cups (600g) cold cooked white long-grain rice
2 tablespoons kecap manis
1 tablespoon light soy sauce
4 spring onions, sliced thinly
1 tablespoon groundnut oil, extra
4 eggs

1   Shell and devein prawns.

2   Heat half the oil in wok; stir-fry sausage, in batches, until browned.

3   Heat remaining oil in wok; stir-fry onion, pepper, chilli, garlic, ginger and paste, until vegetables soften. Add prawns and rice; stir-fry 2 minutes. Return sausage to wok with sauces and half the spring onion; stir-fry until combined.

4   Heat extra oil in large frying pan; fry eggs, one side only, until just set. Divide nasi goreng among serving plates, top each with an egg; sprinkle with remaining spring onion.

pad thai

preparation time 25 minutes ■ cooking time 10 minutes ■
serves 4

540g uncooked medium king prawns

¼ cup (85g) tamarind concentrate

⅓ cup (80ml) sweet chilli sauce

2 tablespoons fish sauce

⅓ cup firmly packed fresh coriander
leaves

¼ cup (35g) roasted unsalted peanuts

¼ cup (20g) fried shallots

2 cups (160g) bean sprouts

4 spring onions, sliced thinly

375g dried rice stick noodles

1 tablespoon groundnut oil

2 cloves garlic, crushed

4cm piece fresh ginger (20g), grated

3 fresh small red thai chillies, chopped
finely

250g minced pork

2 eggs, beaten lightly

1 lime, quartered

1 Shell and devein prawns, leaving tails intact.

2 Combine tamarind and sauces in small jug.

3 Combine coriander, nuts, shallots, half the sprouts and half the
onion in medium bowl.

4 Place noodles in large heatproof bowl, cover with boiling
water; stand until just tender, drain.

5 Meanwhile, heat oil in wok; stir-fry garlic, ginger and chilli
until fragrant. Add pork; stir-fry until cooked. Add prawns; stir-
fry 1 minute. Add egg; stir-fry until set. Add tamarind mixture,
remaining sprouts and onion, and noodles; stir-fry until combined.

6 Divide mixture among serving bowls; sprinkle with coriander
mixture, serve with lime wedges.

sweet soy fried noodles

preparation time 15 minutes ▩ cooking time 20 minutes ▩ serves 4

Known as 'pad sieu' this traditional Thai dish is similar to the famous 'pad thai', but uses kecap manis, a thick, sweet soy sauce, to give it its special flavour. We used a packaged fried tofu, which can be bought from many supermarkets. If you prefer to do it yourself, simply shallow-fry cubes of drained firm silken tofu in vegetable oil until just browned; drain well before tossing with vegetables.

450g fresh wide rice noodles
1 tablespoon groundnut oil
3 cloves garlic, sliced thinly
2 eggs, beaten lightly
280g gai lan, chopped coarsely
200g green beans, cut into 5cm lengths
⅓ cup (80ml) kecap manis
2 tablespoons light soy sauce
½ teaspoon dried chilli flakes
350g packet fried tofu, cut into 2cm cubes
4 spring onions, sliced thinly
¾ cup loosely packed thai basil leaves

1 Place noodles in large heatproof bowl, cover with boiling water; separate with fork, drain.
2 Heat oil in wok; stir-fry garlic until fragrant. Add egg; stir-fry until set. Add vegetables, sauces and chilli; stir-fry until vegetables are tender. Add noodles, tofu, onion and basil; stir-fry until hot.

tomato rice

preparation time 15 minutes ■ cooking time 30 minutes
■ serves 4

2 tablespoons groundnut oil
1 medium brown onion (150g), chopped finely
2 cloves garlic, crushed
3 medium tomatoes (450g), peeled, deseeded, chopped finely
2 tablespoons tomato paste
4 cloves
2 cups (400g) white long-grain rice
3 cups (750ml) water

1 Heat oil in medium saucepan; cook onion, garlic, tomato, paste and cloves, uncovered, about 10 minutes or until mixture is thick and pulpy.
2 Stir in rice and the water; bring to a boil. Reduce heat; cook, covered tightly, over low heat, about 15 minutes or until water is absorbed. Remove from heat; stand, covered, 10 minutes. Fluff rice with fork. Serve sprinkled with coriander, and warmed chapati, if you like.

kaffir lime & rice salad with tofu & cashews

preparation time 20 minutes ■ cooking time 10 minutes
■ serves 4

2 cups (400g) jasmine rice

2 fresh kaffir lime leaves, chopped finely

2 fresh long red chillies, chopped finely

2cm piece fresh ginger (10g), grated

400g packaged marinated tofu pieces, sliced thickly

½ cup coarsely chopped fresh coriander

1 large carrot (180g), cut into matchsticks

3 spring onions, sliced thinly

¾ cup (120g) roasted unsalted cashews, chopped coarsely

lime & palm sugar dressing

1 teaspoon finely grated lime rind

½ cup (125ml) lime juice

2 tablespoons grated palm sugar

2 tablespoons fish sauce

1 Cook rice in large saucepan of boiling water, uncovered, until tender; drain. Rinse under cold water; drain.

2 Meanwhile, make lime and palm sugar dressing.

3 Combine rice, lime leaves, chilli, ginger, tofu, coriander, carrot, half the onion, ½ cup nuts and dressing in large bowl. Serve salad sprinkled with remaining onion and nuts.

lime and palm sugar dressing Combine ingredients in screw-top jar; shake well.

It could be said that there are as many types of biryani as there are grains of rice in this dish; Indians, Pakistanis as well as Bangladeshis all have their own version of biryani. Serve with raita, if you like.

1kg lamb shoulder, cut into 3cm pieces
3cm piece fresh ginger (15g), grated
2 cloves garlic, crushed
2 fresh small red thai chillies, chopped finely
2 teaspoons garam masala
1 tablespoon finely chopped fresh coriander
¼ teaspoon ground turmeric
½ cup (140g) natural yogurt
2 tablespoons ghee
½ cup (40g) flaked almonds
¼ cup (40g) sultanas
2 medium brown onions (300g), sliced thickly
½ cup (125ml) water
pinch saffron threads
1 tablespoon hot milk
1½ cups (300g) basmati rice
¼ cup firmly packed fresh coriander leaves

lamb biryani

preparation time 20 minutes (plus refrigeration time) ■ cooking time 2 hours 15 minutes ■ serves 4

1 Combine lamb, ginger, garlic, chilli, garam masala, chopped coriander, turmeric and yogurt in medium bowl, cover; refrigerate overnight.

2 Heat half the ghee in large saucepan; cook nuts and sultanas, stirring, until nuts brown lightly. Remove from pan.

3 Heat remaining ghee in same pan; cook onion, covered, 5 minutes. Uncover; cook, stirring occasionally, about 5 minutes or until browned lightly. Reserve half of the onion.

4 Add lamb mixture to pan; cook, stirring, until browned. Add the water; bring to a boil. Reduce heat; simmer, covered, 1 hour. Uncover; simmer about 30 minutes or until lamb is tender and sauce is thickened.

5 Meanwhile, combine saffron and milk in small bowl; stand 15 minutes.

6 Cook rice in medium saucepan of boiling water, uncovered, 5 minutes; drain.

7 Preheat oven to 180°C/160°C fan-assisted.

8 Spread half the lamb mixture into oiled deep 2-litre (8-cup) ovenproof dish. Layer with half the rice; top with remaining lamb mixture then remaining rice. Drizzle milk mixture over rice; cover tightly with greased foil and lid. Bake about 30 minutes or until rice is tender.

9 Serve biryani topped with reserved onion, nut and sultana mixture and coriander.

spinach pilau

preparation time 10 minutes ■ cooking time 15 minutes ■ serves 4 to 6

2 tablespoons vegetable oil

6 spring onions, sliced

2 dried red chillies, crushed

½ teaspoon coriander seeds

1 clove garlic, crushed

2 cups (400g) long-grain rice

1 litre (4 cups) water

1 tablespoon chicken stock powder

500g spinach, chopped

¼ cup chopped fresh basil

½ cup (125ml) natural yogurt

1   Heat vegetable oil in medium saucepan; cook onions, chillies, seeds and garlic, stirring, until fragrant.

2   Stir in rice; add water and stock powder. Boil; immediately simmer, covered, 15 minutes or until rice is tender and liquid absorbed.

3   Remove from heat; stir in spinach, basil and yogurt.

lemon & saffron rice

preparation time 10 minutes (plus standing time)
■ cooking time 15 minutes ■ serves 4 to 6

1 litre (4 cups) chicken stock

¼ teaspoon saffron threads

2 tablespoons ghee

2 small onions (160g), sliced

2 cloves garlic, crushed

1 teaspoon grated fresh ginger

6 curry leaves

2 teaspoons grated lemon rind

2 cups (400g) basmati rice, washed, drained

¼ cup (60ml) lemon juice

¼ cup chopped fresh coriander

1 Bring stock to boil in medium saucepan, remove from heat, stir in saffron; cover, stand 15 minutes.

2 Heat ghee in medium saucepan; cook onions, garlic, ginger and curry leaves, stirring, until onions are browned lightly. Stir in rind and rice.

3 Add stock to rice mixture; simmer, covered, 15 minutes or until rice is tender and liquid absorbed. Stir in juice and fresh coriander; stand, covered, 5 minutes.

caramelised onion, fruit & nut pilau

preparation time 10 minutes ■ cooking time 30 minutes ■ serves 4 to 6

2 tablespoons ghee

2 large onions (400g), sliced

2 tablespoons ghee, extra

1 teaspoon hot chilli powder

1 teaspoon ground black pepper

¼ teaspoon saffron threads

4 cardamom pods, bruised

4 cloves

1 cinnamon stick

1 teaspoon salt

2 cups (400g) basmati rice, washed, drained

1 litre (4 cups) water

½ cup (75g) currants

½ cup (75g) chopped dried apricots

½ cup (80g) sultanas

½ cup (70g) slivered almonds, toasted

1   Heat ghee in large saucepan; cook onions, stirring, 15 minutes or until caramelised. Remove from pan.

2   Add extra ghee and spices to same pan; cook, stirring until fragrant. Stir in salt, rice and onions.

3   Add water; boil, then immediately simmer, covered, 10 minutes or until rice is tender and water absorbed. Stir in currants, apricots and sultanas; stand, covered, 5 minutes. Just before serving, stir in nuts.

khitcherie

preparation time 10 minutes (plus soaking time)
■ cooking time 25 minutes ■ serves 4 to 6

1 cup (200g) toor dhal (yellow
split peas)
3 tablespoons ghee
1 medium onion (150g),
chopped finely
2 cloves garlic, crushed
2 small green chillies,
chopped finely
2 teaspoons finely grated
fresh ginger
½ teaspoon ground turmeric
1 teaspoon cumin seeds

½ teaspoon garam masala
1 teaspoon ground coriander
1 cinnamon stick
4 curry leaves
2 teaspoons salt
1½ cups (300g) basmati rice,
washed, drained
1 cup (170g) raisins
1 litre (4 cups) hot water
1 tablespoon lime juice
½ cup (75g) cashews,
toasted

1 Place dhal in small bowl, cover with cold water; soak
1 hour. Drain well.
2 Heat ghee in medium saucepan; cook onion, garlic,
chillies, ginger, spices, curry leaves and salt, stirring, until
onion is browned lightly and mixture fragrant.
3 Add dhal, rice, raisins and water; boil, then immediately
simmer, covered, 15 minutes or until rice is tender. Remove
from heat, discard cinnamon, stir in juice; stand, covered,
5 minutes. Just before serving, stir in cashews.

2 tablespoons ghee
2 medium onions (300g), sliced thinly
2 medium potatoes (400g), chopped
1 teaspoon cumin seeds
2 cups (400g) long-grain rice
1 litre (4 cups) water
1 cup (125g) frozen peas

mint masala

½ cup firmly packed fresh mint leaves
2 long green chillies, chopped
2 tablespoons vegetable oil
½ teaspoon garam masala
1 teaspoon salt
¼ cup (35g) coconut milk powder
¼ cup (60ml) water

nawabi biryani

preparation time 15 minutes ■ cooking time 20 minutes (plus standing time) ■ serves 4 to 6

1   Heat ghee in large saucepan; cook onions and potatoes, stirring, until both are just browned lightly.

2   Blend or process all mint masala ingredients until pureed.

3   Add cumin seeds and mint masala to pan; cook, stirring, until fragrant. Stir in rice.

4   Add water to pan; simmer, covered, 10 minutes. Remove from heat, stir in peas; stand, covered, 10 minutes.

glossary

beans

black an earthy-flavoured dried bean; also known as turtle beans or black kidney beans.

black-eyed also known as black-eyed peas, are the dried seed of a variant of the snake or yard bean.

borlotti also known as roman beans, they can be eaten fresh or dried. Are a pale pink or beige colour with darker red spots.

kidney medium-size red bean, slightly floury in texture yet sweet in flavour; sold dried or canned, it is found in bean mixes and is used in chile con carne.

pinto similar to borlotti, a plump, kidney-shaped, pinky beige bean speckled with brown to red streaks; available canned or dried.

besan flour made from ground chickpeas; also known as garam flour or chickpea flour.

cardamom native to India and used extensively in its cooking; can be purchased in pod, seed or ground form. Has an aromatic, distinctive, sweetly rich taste, and is one of the world's most expensive spices.

chilli available in many different types and sizes. Use rubber gloves when chopping fresh chillies as they can burn your skin. Removing seeds and membranes decreases the heat level

chipotle chillies also known as ahumado chillies, they are dried, smoked jalapeños. They have a deeply intense smoky flavour rather than a blast of heat. They average 6cm in length and are dark brown, almost black.

green any unripened chilli; also some particular varieties that are ripe when green, such as jalapeño, habanero, poblano or serrano.

flakes, dried deep-red dehydrated very fine slices and whole seeds; good for cooking or for sprinkling over already-cooked food.

jalapeños pronounced hah-lah-pain-yo. Fairly hot, green chillies, available bottled in brine or fresh from greengrocers.

thai red small, medium hot, and bright red in colour.

chinese cabbage also known as wombok, peking cabbage, wong bok or petsai. Elongated in shape with pale green, crinkly leaves.

chorizo sausage of Spanish origin, made of coarsely ground pork and highly seasoned with garlic and chilli.

coconut

cream available in cans and cartons; made from coconut and water.

desiccated unsweetened concentrated, dried shredded coconut.

milk pure, unsweetened coconut milk available in cans.

milk powder coconut milk that has been dehydrated and ground to a fine powder.

coriander also known as dhania, cilantro or chinese parsley; bright-green leafed herb with a pungent flavour. Also available ground and in seed form; roots and stems can also be used.

cumin also known as zeera; related to the parsley family. Has a spicy, nutty flavour. Available in seed form or dried and ground.

curry leaves bright-green, shiny, sharp-ended leaves having a flavour similar to traditional curry powders, hence their name; are used fresh or dried.

daikon is an everyday fixture at the Japanese table; this long, white horseradish has a wonderful, sweet flavour; buy those that are firm and unwrinkled from Asian food stores.

dhal legumes such as lentils, dried peas and beans.

channa also known as chickpeas or garbanzos; see CHICKPEAS.

masoor also known as red lentils.

moong also known as split mung beans, these are the same pale-yellow pulse used to make bean sprouts.

enchiladas baked tortillas stuffed with beans, cheese and sour cream.

gai lan is a member of the cabbage family, and is also known as chinese kale, chinese broccoli and gai larn; this green vegetable is appreciated more for its stems than its coarse leaves. It is similar in texture to regular broccoli, but milder in taste.

galangal also known as ka or lengkaus if fresh and laos if dried and powdered. A rhizome with a hot ginger-citrusy flavour; it looks like ginger but is dense and fibrous and harder to cut.

garam masala a combination of powdered spices, consisting of cardamom, cinnamon, cloves, coriander, cumin and nutmeg in varying proportions. Sometimes black pepper is used to make a hot variation.

ghee a pure butter fat available in cans; can be heated to high temperatures without burning due to its lack of salt and milk solids.

ginger

fresh, green or root scrape away skin and grate, chop or slice as required.

ground should not be substituted for fresh ginger in any recipe.

herbs we have specified when to use fresh or dried herbs. Use dried (not ground) herbs in the proportion of 1:4 for fresh herbs, eg. 1 teaspoon dried herbs instead of 4 teaspoons (1 tablespoon) chopped fresh herbs.

jaggery also known as gur; a moulded lump sugar made from either distilled sugarcane or palm juice. Available from Asian specialty shops; substitute dark brown sugar.

kaffir lime leaves also known as bai magrood; look like two glossy dark-green leaves joined end to end, forming a rounded hourglass shape. Used fresh or dried, like bay leaves or curry leaves, in many Asian dishes. Sold fresh, dried or frozen, the dried leaves are less potent so double the number called for in a recipe if you substitute them for fresh leaves. A strip of fresh lime peel may be substituted for each kaffir lime leaf.

lemongrass also known as takrai, serai or serah. A tall, clumping, lemon-smelling and tasting, sharp-edged aromatic tropical grass; the white lower part of the stem is used, finely chopped, in much of the cooking of South-East Asia. Can be found, fresh, dried, powdered and frozen, in supermarkets and greengrocers, as well as Asian food stores.

lentils dried pulses. There are many different varieties of lentils, usually identified and named after their colour, such as red, brown and yellow (split peas).

masala literally meaning blended spices; a masala can be whole spices, a paste or powder, and can include herbs as well as spices and other seasonings. Traditional dishes are usually based on and named after particular masalas.

mustard seeds can be black or yellow.

nigella seeds also known as black onion seeds or kalonji.

oil

corn an odourless, bland oil, obtained from corn kernels; has a high smoke point.

groundnut pressed from ground peanuts; used frequently in stir-frying because of its high smoke point.

sesame made from roasted, crushed white sesame seeds; used as a flavouring rather than a cooking medium.

vegetable any of a wide number of oils having a plant, rather than an animal, source. We used a polyunsaturated vegetable oil.

okra a green, ridged, immature seed pod, also known as lady's fingers.

Pak choy also known as bok choy, pak choi, chinese white cabbage or chinese chard; has a fresh, mild mustard taste. Use both stems and leaves, stir-fried or braised. Baby pak choy, also known as pak kat farang or shanghai bok choy, is much smaller and more tender than pak choy.

panch phora a combination of five aromatic seeds — mustard, fennel, cumin, fenugreek and nigella (black onion) — fried in hot oil before use in various dishes.

paneer a simple, delicate fresh cheese used as a major source of protein in the Indian diet; substitute it with ricotta.

pappadums sun-dried wafers made from a combination of lentil and rice flours, oil and spices; shallow- or deep-fry, or microwave, to reconstitute. Eaten on their own as a snack, with pickles and chutneys, or crumbled.

paprika ground dried peppers; sweet or hot.

saag the Indian name for spinach; also known as palak.

saffron stigma of a member of crocus family, available in strands or ground form; imparts a yellow-orange colour to food once infused. Quality varies greatly; the best is the most expensive spice in the world. Store in freezer.

salsa a chunky sauce served as an accompaniment, often based on tomato, chilli, garlic and onion. May be cooked or uncooked, mild or very spicy.

star anise the dried star-shaped pod of an evergreen tree, it has an aniseed flavour.

taco a folded tortilla that has been fried until crisp; tacos are used as a container for spicy meat fillings.

thai basil is also known as horapa; it's different from holy basil and sweet basil in both look and taste, having smaller leaves and purplish stems. It has a slight aniseed taste; available from Asian food stores, some specialist fruit and vegetable shops and supermarkets.

tortilla thin, round unleavened bread originating in Mexico. Made from either wheat flour or corn. Can be fried to make crisp taco shells, stuffed with beans, sour cream and cheese and baked (enchiladas), torn into strips and fried to make scoops for salsas (tostaditas), or fried and stacked one on top of the other with a filling placed

turmeric also known as kamin; is a rhizome related to galangal and ginger, must be grated or pounded to release its somewhat acrid aroma and pungent flavour. Known for the golden colour it imparts to dishes. Fresh turmeric can be substituted with the more common dried powder (use 2 teaspoons of ground turmeric plus a teaspoon of sugar for every 20g of fresh turmeric called for in a recipe).

vietnamese mint is not a mint at all, but a pungent and peppery narrow-leafed member of the buckwheat family. Not confined to Vietnam, it is also known as cambodian mint, pak pai (Thailand), laksa leaf (Indonesia), daun kesom (Singapore), and rau ram in Vietnam. It is a common ingredient in Asian foods, particularly soups, salads and stir-fries.

index

conversion charts

Measures

The cup and spoon measurements used in this book are metric: one measuring cup holds approximately 250ml; one metric tablespoon holds 20ml; one metric teaspoon holds 5ml.

All cup and spoon measurements are level. The most accurate way of measuring dry ingredients is to weigh them. When measuring liquids, use a clear glass or plastic jug with metric markings. We use large eggs with an average weight of 60g.

Liquid measures

metric	imperial
30ml	1 fl oz
60ml	2 fl oz
100ml	3 fl oz
125ml	4 fl oz
150ml	5 fl oz (¼ pint/1 gill)
190ml	6 fl oz
250ml	8 fl oz
300ml	10 fl oz (½pt)
500ml	16 fl oz
600ml	20 fl oz (1 pint)
1000ml (1 litre)	1¾pints

Dry measures

metric	imperial
15g	½oz
30g	1oz
60g	2oz
90g	3oz
125g	4oz (¼lb)
155g	5oz
185g	6oz
220g	7oz
250g	8oz (½lb)
280g	9oz
315g	10oz
345g	11oz
375g	12oz (¾lb)
410g	13oz
440g	14oz
470g	15oz
500g	16oz (1lb)
750g	24oz (1½lb)
1kg	32oz (2lb)

Length measures

metric	imperial
3mm	⅛in
6mm	¼in
1cm	½in
2cm	¾in
2.5cm	1in
5cm	2in
6cm	2½in
8cm	3in
10cm	4in
13cm	5in
15cm	6in
18cm	7in
20cm	8in
23cm	9in
25cm	10in
28cm	11in
30cm	12in (1ft)

Oven temperatures

These oven temperatures are only a guide for conventional ovens. For fan-assisted ovens, check the manufacturer's manual.

	°C (Celcius)	°F (Fahrenheit)	gas mark
Very low	120	250	½
Low	150	275-300	1-2
Moderately low	170	325	3
Moderate	180	350-375	4-5
Moderately hot	200	400	6
Hot	220	425-450	7-8
Very hot	240	475	9

WARNING This book contains recipes for dishes made with raw or lightly cooked eggs. These should be avoided by vulnerable people such as pregnant and nursing mothers, invalids, the elderly, babies and young children.